BUILDING CAREER CONNECTIONS

Networking Tools for Law Students and New Lawyers

By Donna Gerson

Suite 1110
1025 Connecticut Avenue NW
Washington, DC 20036-5413
(202) 835-1001 — Fax (202) 835-1112
www.nalp.org
Additional websites: www.nalpdirectory.com — www.pslawnet.org —
www.nalplawschoolsonline.org

ISBN 978-1-55733-052-9

Contents

Preface 5

Chapter 1: What Is Networking? 9
What Networking Is Not 11
Why Networking Is Important for Your Career Development . . .12
Stop Making Excuses! – Rebutting Popular Misconceptions about Networking 13

Chapter 2: How Do I Network? 19
Identify Your Personal Network 19
Broaden Your Networking Circle Beyond Personal Contacts 22
Worksheet: My Personal Network 32

Chapter 3: Socializing and Networking 35
Thriving on the Social Circuit 35
In Their Own Words: Connecting in Unlikely Places 36
Sidebar: Business Card Etiquette 41
A Crash Course in Conversation Skills 42
The Three S's of Conversations 42
Tackling "Table Talk" Programs 43
Sidebar: Secrets of Good Conversation from the Experts 45
Conversation Starters 45
Conversation Enders 46
In Their Own Words: Tips for Starting and Ending Conversations 47
Conversation Killers 48
Networking to Fit Your Style 48
The Party's Over: Making the Individual Approach 50
Sidebar: Telephone Etiquette 54
Successful Meeting Tips 54
Sidebar: Picking Up the Check – Who Pays the Tab? 54
Dealing with Rejection ... or When to Call It Quits 55
In Their Own Words: Showing Up 56
Worksheet: Sample Networking Log 57

Chapter 4: Informational Interviewing .59
What Is Informational Interviewing? .59
Getting Started .62
Identifying More Sources .63
Making the Approach .65
Prepare for Your Informational Interview .68
The Interview .68
Follow-up .69
In Their Own Words: Trust These Time-Tested Job Search Strategies .70
Cultivation .71
In Their Own Words: A First-hand Experience with Informational Interviewing .71

Chapter 5: Networking for Business Development and Career Growth .73
Strategies to Build Your Network .74
In Their Own Words: Creating a Mentoring Network .76
In Their Own Words: Lessons Learned by Successful Women Lawyers .81
Schedule Your Networking Efforts .84
Follow-up .86
In Their Own Words: Networking Tips for Women .88
In Their Own Words: Staying Networked .89

Chapter 6: Networking and the Nontraditional Legal Career .91
In Their Own Words: Networking and the Nontraditional Job Search .97

Epilogue .99

Bibliography .100

Acknowledgments .103

About the Author .103

About NALP .104

PREFACE

When I was a college junior living in Philadelphia and pondering my future, my mother called to tell me about a lawyer she had heard about in Center City. The lawyer was a friend of a friend; he didn't know my mother at all. "Call Gary Gittelman," urged my mother. "He'd be happy to speak with you about legal careers," she said. "Why should I call a total stranger?" I grumbled. "Why would a partner at a law firm, a successful adult, want to waste a minute with a college student who is considering law school?"

I procrastinated for several weeks, but finally relented and called Gary. As I stammered through an explanation for my call, Gary graciously invited me to visit his office. Several days later, attired in a suit and heels, I took the bus downtown and toured my very first law office. Gary's firm specialized in insurance defense litigation, a field I had never heard of before. Frankly, aside from a high school internship with the local district attorney's office, I knew nothing about the law. I spent the day with Gary and observed my first deposition, learned about how cases get settled, and saw a law office in action. While I felt nervous and out of place, I did learn a great deal and generally enjoyed the experience. After writing a thank you note to Gary, I returned to campus and promptly forgot about Gary and his firm.

Fast-forward to the first semester of my first year of law school. Nearly everyone in my class was scrambling for a paid summer position with a law firm, a difficult feat for any first-year law student to achieve. Having worked as a corporate paralegal between college and law school, I had a slight advantage over my classmates, but no family connections to speak of.

I researched Philadelphia law firms and mailed letters to a variety of large and mid-size firms. To my surprise, I received a letter from a firm asking me to schedule an interview. After scheduling the interview, I began to research the firm more carefully. As I glanced at the list of attorney names in Martindale-Hubbell®, one looked vaguely familiar – Gary Gittelman. Why did I know that name? Of course, he was the lawyer who invited me to visit his firm several years earlier.

I interviewed at the law firm and things seemed to go well. During my final interview with a partner, I casually mentioned that I had visited the firm several years earlier and asked to be remembered to Gary Gittelman. "Do you know Gary?" asked the partner. I was in a bit of a jam here. I didn't really know Gary, I had just taken up a very kind offer from him at the behest of my mother. I didn't think I would recognize Gary if I ran into him in the hall. "Well," I replied, "he showed me around for a day when I was a college student and he was a really super person. Please let him know that I did go to law school and that he influenced my decision." "I'd take you to his office right now, but he's at a deposition today," replied the partner.

A few days later, I received a call from the firm offering me a paid summer position. The firm's policy was to assign summer associates to work with specific partner teams and my partner would be Gary Gittelman. Apparently, my brief visit as a college student followed by a serendipitous name-drop helped me get an inside track in a competitive job market. I was probably one of a dozen classmates who found paid employment with a firm following my first year of law school.

Mother was right about going outside my comfort zone and contacting a stranger. From that day forward, I became convinced that my success hinged not only on my accomplishments but also on my circle of friends and acquaintances; I was dependent upon a combination of what I knew *and* who I knew. Thenceforth, networking would play an important role in my career and personal life.

By reading this book, you are demonstrating a desire to learn and grow both professionally and personally. This book will address the key issues that law students and lawyers need to know about networking for professional and personal success. From a working definition of networking to step-by-step instructions on how to cultivate and steward relationships, this book will give you the tools you need to succeed. You will learn how to:

- Identify networking sources
- Initiate contacts
- Socialize with confidence
- Develop and nurture networking relationships
- Continuously broaden your circle of contacts
- Arrange and conduct informational interviews

Take these ideas, incorporate what works for you, and use the power of networking and informational interviewing to enhance your professional opportunities and leverage the value of your law degree. Your efforts will be rewarded, not just professionally but personally, as you engage more fully in building and inhabiting your own personal community.

Chapter 1

What Is Networking?

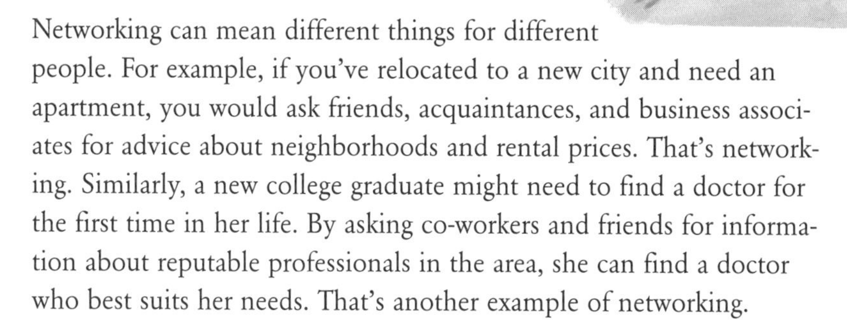

Networking is the process by which an individual gathers information and, in turn, shares information with others, creating and enhancing connections for mutual benefit.

Networking can mean different things for different people. For example, if you've relocated to a new city and need an apartment, you would ask friends, acquaintances, and business associates for advice about neighborhoods and rental prices. That's networking. Similarly, a new college graduate might need to find a doctor for the first time in her life. By asking co-workers and friends for information about reputable professionals in the area, she can find a doctor who best suits her needs. That's another example of networking.

"Networking is not only a means to get business. It's an easy, efficient means to get information," says Colleen Davis, president and CEO of Aim to Succeed (www.womenbizleaders.com), a Twin Cities-based networking organization. "You can tap into your network to find and get essentially anything you want or need."

For law students, the networking process will focus on finding a job and issues related to career development. Later in one's career, networking will take on significance as a means to obtain clients, develop business, and market your law firm.

When networking, you can expect the following from your sources:

- General information about career opportunities
- The inside scoop on a particular legal market (mergers, dissolutions, hiring trends)
- Referrals to others who might assist you in your job search
- Feedback about résumés and cover letters
- Ideas about job search strategies

- Guidance on employer personalities and workplace environments
- Moral support
- Professional and personal mentoring

When developing your professional and personal network, assume a long-term outlook on the process. Networking should not be viewed as a "once-and-done" assignment to produce a single result. To the contrary, networking ought to be approached as a process that develops over time; in many cases, networking contacts grow and blossom over the course of a career, or better still, a life. "Networking is about forming and forging relationships that last over time," observes Judy Rosemarin, founder and president of Sense-Able Strategies, Inc., a New York-based career coaching firm.

> No man is an island entire of itself, each man is a piece of the continent, a part of the main.
>
> — JOHN DONNE

Moreover, networking is not simply an exercise in collecting the names of significant people for your Rolodex. Anyone can research names and phone numbers. The key to realizing the benefits of that research is building connections and learning new and more complete information that will enable you to make informed, intelligent decisions about your career. In the case of a law student seeking a job in a particular practice area, networking means learning about the intricacies of practice in that niche by leveraging relationships with people who have contact with the domain. For a lawyer contemplating a move to the West Coast, networking will help garner inside information about the significant law firms and lawyers in that area, the economic forecast for a target locale, and other relevant information pertaining to the pending relocation.

Networking is all about connecting with others and sharing information for mutual benefit. These connections will typically take the form of conversations. Marc Karasu, a career counselor and vice president of Yahoo HotJobs, a job search website, explains that "networking, simply put, is conversations held with friends, family, colleagues, and others that help you gather information that could be helpful to your job search."

What Networking Is Not

Networking gets a bad reputation from those who do not honor the process of meeting, learning, and sharing with others. Over the years, I have heard law students describe networking in negative terms, including "cheesy," "déclassé," and "humiliating." Others dismiss networking as "using people." Remember, those who simply use people to extract information or for name-dropping purposes are not networking in good faith.

Networking is *not* about:

- Asking for a job
- Bragging
- Gossiping about others
- Bullying or threatening
- Using people
- Pretending to be someone you are not
- Imposing your will on others

Networking is the process by which an individual gathers information and, in turn, shares information with others, creating and enhancing connections for mutual benefit.

Focus on the reciprocal nature of the networking process – the interpersonal give and take. One law student expressed her comfort with networking by explaining that once she herself experienced the pleasure of helping another person acquire information, she stopped worrying about her concerns about asking for help. "It feels good to help and it empowers me," she explained. "I know that sometimes I'll be asking for help and other times I'll be offering assistance."

Attorney Kevin Grierson, a patent attorney in Norfolk, Virginia, reiterates this point: "If you develop a reputation for helping other people meet their needs, people will naturally start turning to you to help solve their problems – and solving problems (whether before or after they appear) is, at bottom, what your job will be as a lawyer."

While you may be on the asking end of the networking equation today, you will certainly do your share of imparting information later in your career. Commit to this philosophy today, and you will ultimately gain a comfort level with the process of connecting and sharing that we call networking.

Why Networking Is Important for Your Career Development

Networking is the means by which most law students will find employment, particularly full-time employment following graduation. On-campus interviews, which reward top grades and high academic achievement, account for a minuscule percentage of jobs. Most law students find jobs either through networking or self-initiated contact with prospective employers, often a combination of the two.

Networking will help you discover the hidden job market and learn about work opportunities that may never be published. A large percentage of available jobs are not advertised; instead they are filled by word-of-mouth. Even those jobs that are advertised are often filled with a candidate who somehow made a personal connection with the employer. As a result, those who are "in the know" and are connected to a network of contacts who know about their skills and interests will be in a position to benefit when their contacts learn about an opening through the informal grapevine.

> "The future belc to those who believe in the beauty of the dreams."
>
> — ELEANOR ROOSEVELT

Beyond finding a job directly following graduation, networking skills will aid you throughout your career. Your first job out of law school will almost certainly not be your last. Recent studies of associate turnover rates reveal that, within the first two years following graduation, nearly a quarter of the associates at law firms of all sizes have moved on to other jobs. After five years, more than half of those hired out of law school have left their original firms. *(Keeping the Keepers II: Mobility and Management of Associates,* The NALP Foundation for Law Career Research and

Education, 2003.) Moving between jobs is both common and expected in the legal profession. Building and maintaining a strong network of contacts will enable you to learn about promising opportunities later in your career.

Networking will also influence your ability to attract and retain clients. Developing your own client base (commonly known as "rainmaking") will impact your rate of compensation and your role in your firm and local legal community. Many law students and new attorneys assume that rainmakers are born, not made. Not so. Those lawyers who are committed to developing a book of business are also top-notch networkers who understand that cultivating relationships (as well as delivering effective legal counsel) results in a growing clientele.

Stop Making Excuses! — Rebutting Popular Misconceptions about Networking

Why don't more law students and new lawyers engage in networking? Excuses abound for failing to learn and utilize these skills. Some law students and new lawyers express a fear of rejection. Others operate from a sense of entitlement that a law degree ought to guarantee job opportunities along with a high level of social status and professional stability. Still others rely on the on-campus interview process, even though statistics show that few law students actually find full-time jobs through this system. After graduation, many new lawyers are surprised to learn that most lateral jobs are never posted and the primary means of finding new positions derives from the hidden market of personal connections.

Here are some of the most common excuses I have heard over the years, and the rebuttals that refute these misconceptions:

Excuse #1: Asking for help shows weakness. Some law students fear appearing to be stupid or misinformed in a networking situation. To avoid the risk of appearing unknowledgeable, they will proceed in ignorance rather than learn from a more experienced individual.

Rebuttal: No one can be an expert in all areas of law and practice development, particularly early in one's career. As a law student or someone who is at the beginning of your legal practice, your job is to absorb information and learn from as many sources as possible. While it's helpful to read books and articles that pertain to career development, there is no substitute for asking questions from someone more experienced.

> Alone we can do so llittle, together we ca[n] do so much.
>
> — HELEN KELLER

Asking for help is not a sign of weakness; rather, asking indicates a level of curiosity, motivation, and enthusiasm for the future. "It's difficult if not impossible for most fledgling legal eagles to launch a successful career on their own straight out of law school," writes Martha Neil, legal affairs writer for the *ABA Journal.* "But by forming alliances with more experienced attorneys, they can learn what they need to know to establish themselves in the profession and prove their value to their employers."

Being asked to offer advice confers a sense of power and responsibility that most professionals I spoke with welcome. Don't assume that people will feel put upon if solicited for advice; in many instances they will feel empowered and grateful to be of assistance. And remember, when it's your turn to offer advice and information, be gracious about your time and share your wisdom.

Excuse #2: I'm afraid of rejection. Students and new lawyers will avoid approaching potential networking contacts because they fear being ignored or dismissed. "What if I ask and don't get a response?"

Rebuttal: Rejection is part and parcel of both the job search and client development process. The sooner you understand that a rebuff is seldom a rebuke and is not personal in nature, the more effective you will become in rebounding and refocusing your energies. "The most significant impediment law students face when networking is their own fear," observes Erin Binns, Assistant Director of Career Services at Marquette Law School in Milwaukee.

Some law students will receive a negative response from a networking contact and then proceed to sulk for weeks on end about the lost opportunities and the sense of personal failure they are experiencing. While it's normal to feel badly when an opportunity is lost, the most successful networkers (and job seekers) maintain a level of resilience and a positive outlook that enables them to learn from their mistakes and forge ahead.

Networking involves asking; sometimes the answer will be "yes" and occasionally the answer (or non-answer) will be "no," but every question produces one answer or another, and thus advances the cause of the person who asks. The trick to being a successful networker is taking the negative responses in stride and moving ahead. There is no guarantee that you will be successful 100 percent of the time as you approach individuals for information and advice. At times you will initiate contact and you will receive no response whatsoever. Or you may meet a potential source of information and find that they cannot provide you with the information or contacts you desire. Ultimately, the most successful networkers understand that patience and persistence are the most valuable allies in this long-term process and that constantly asking means constantly moving forward.

Excuse #3: The "Ick" Factor. Law students who avoid networking describe the process in negative terms, such as "using" people or employing "false pretenses" to get ahead.

Rebuttal: Networking is a give-and-take process that empowers others to share information and ideas for mutual benefit. While you may not be in a position to offer career advice today, you can share other helpful information, from the newest restaurant in town to a book recommendation to an insight about college or law school. Ask with the expectation of reciprocating, if not in kind then in context.

Excuse #4: I Don't Have Time to Network. I have heard law students explain that networking is too time-consuming a process to be incorporated into their busy lives. Between classes, exams, and attempts to hang onto a bit of social life, law students find themselves strapped for time, and job searching falls to the bottom of the priority list. I hear law students say, "I'd rather just apply for jobs that are posted and see what happens. At least I know there's a job opening when a job is posted." Others say, "I'd rather find my job through on-campus interviewing (OCI) because the process is quick and I get it over with in the fall."

> Vision is the art seeing things invisible.
>
> — JONATHAN SW

Rebuttal: Relatively few full-time jobs are found through OCI. Even if you do secure employment following graduation through OCI, subsequent job searches after graduation will, almost invariably, involve outreach beyond simply submitting a résumé electronically. Learning the networking skills necessary to gather career information will benefit you, regardless of your credentials, following graduation.

Most jobs are filled through word-of-mouth and are never advertised. By failing to network, you miss out on a large segment of the hidden job market. Furthermore, even those jobs that are posted are often filled with a candidate who somehow made a personal connection with the employer. Therefore, making the time to network offers the long-term benefit of positioning you to make that golden personal connection.

Savvy law students make time during law school to reach out and connect with professionals. In chapter 2, you will discover avenues to network that can be found right on your law school campus as well as, for more adventurous souls, those that lie beyond the confines of your law school.

Excuse #5: I'm Shy. Networking is only for socially gregarious types who enjoy parties and being the center of attention.

Rebuttal: Networking involves connecting with others; these connections can be achieved just as easily (if not more easily) through quiet conversations, e-mail exchanges, or one-on-one meetings as they can through large gatherings. The best networkers are not necessarily the extroverted, gregarious types; the best networkers tend to be good listeners who enjoy connecting with people and follow through.

If you detest large networking events, then learn to create opportunities that will enable you to connect on your own terms. In chapter 3, you will learn networking strategies for law students who may feel uncomfortable in large social settings.

Excuse #6: Bragging Is Impolite. Many law students confuse networking with boasting about one's achievements or exploiting existing connections for selfish ends.

Rebuttal: As children, most of us were taught not to brag. As a result, some people confuse sharing information about one's relevant achievements with boastfulness. When connecting with others, you may have information, skills, or knowledge that would be valued by the other person. In these instances, sharing information about one's credentials will benefit both parties. Why keep it a secret that you won "best brief" in the appellate moot court competition? Why not describe to a potential contact that you are participating in your school's family law clinic and just successfully argued a motion before a trial court judge? Sharing information about your skills and interests will help you make valuable connections.

Excuse #7: I Never Learned How to Network. Too many students believe the myth that a law degree entitles a graduate to the job of his or her dreams at a six-figure starting salary. After all, after so many years of studying and achievement, shouldn't a law degree guarantee career success? As a result, many law students rely not only on the OCI process (which is limited and flawed), but also on computer databases, job posting boards, and paid placement services to find the perfect job. The right job, they assume, will simply appear. As a result, they never learn the skills necessary to become effective networkers.

Rebuttal: Networking is a learned skill, and the good news is that you can start learning and practicing today. Timothy E. Parks, Director of Business Development for the Business & Finance Practice Group at Morgan, Lewis & Bockius LLP, one of the largest law firms in the U.S., teaches lawyers how to network and develop business. "We emphasize a concrete series of actions and approaches that transform networking from a mystery into a process. These are skills that every lawyer ought to study and cultivate," Parks notes.

Law students, too, can develop, practice, and perfect the skills necessary to connect with others and forge ahead in their careers. Chapter 2 will explore the details of how to make these connections and develop a style that works best for you.

Chapter 2

How Do I Network?

Now that you understand the importance of networking and how it impacts your job search and career, you can take tangible steps to achieve your goal of connecting with others. Getting started can be a challenge. You confront a vast universe of networking possibilities with no road map to guide you toward your goal.

This chapter will supply a step-by-step guide to becoming a confident networker. For some individuals, networking is a natural extension of their personal lives; for others, the skills must be learned, used, and reinforced. Don't approach this challenge as an "all or nothing" proposition. Begin slowly by trying different tactics and finding what works best for you.

Identify Your Personal Network

Begin with the assumption that everyone is a possible information source, from your hair stylist to your dog-sitter: Operate under the theory that "you never know who someone might know." Many law students assume that there is one perfect source for the important information they seek when, in reality, you will cull advice and information from a variety of sources over time. Do not write off anyone in your circle of acquaintances and friends simply because you assume they are not knowledgeable.

Share your career goals with your family and tap into the network that may be right at your dinner table. Remember that networking can start with a simple request for someone's advice or opinion. This can be difficult for some law students who believe that they need to secure employment without any intervention, particularly from family members. In a competitive job market, you need all the assistance at your disposal. If that means asking your great uncle for advice, then go ahead. The results may surprise you.

One law student shared the following story with me: His father and uncle were estranged over a long-standing family dispute. Despite the tension, the uncle and his nephew, the law student, maintained contact over the years. His uncle was a very successful businessman with many contacts throughout the city. The law student sought a job in business law following graduation and was experiencing difficulty making contacts. Cautiously, he approached his uncle and asked for help. The uncle was pleased to arrange several appointments for his nephew, one of which ultimately led to a full-time job offer.

Attorney Kristen McManus Powers, formerly with Catholic University's Career Services Office and currently Career Development Manager at Arnold & Porter LLP in Washington, D.C., recalls a law student who desperately wanted to land a federal clerkship following graduation. Powers suggested that the law student mention her career goal to literally anyone she encountered. While visiting her dentist for a routine checkup, the law student described her interest in clerking after graduation. "My brother-in-law is a federal judge in Virginia. Maybe he could help," the dentist responded. It turns out that the dentist's brother-in-law was the chief judge in Alexandria and he ended up hiring the law student.

Consider the story of another Washington, D.C., area law school graduate who lamented to his career counselor that he had no connections that would enable him to secure a clerkship with a federal appellate judge following graduation. Following the "tell everyone you know" rule, he happened to mention his clerkship aspirations to one of his aunts over the holidays. His aunt said that her best friend's husband was a judge, but she had no idea what court he sat on. The following week, the aunt called her nephew (the law student) to tell him that her friend's husband was a judge for the U.S. Court of Appeals for the Fifth Circuit. Would he like to be introduced to the judge? asked the aunt. The judge needed to attend a judicial conference in Washington, D.C. the following month. The law student was able to give the judge and his wife a tour of the nation's capital and – happy ending – he was offered a clerkship position.

"Concentrate on the people who are already part of your existing network," advises Keith Ferrazzi, author of *Never Eat Alone* (Doubleday, 2005). To get you started, here is a checklist of **personal contacts** that you might consider tapping as you begin to network:

- Parents
- Siblings
- Grandparents
- Extended family (uncles, aunts, cousins)
- All of your spouse's or partner's relatives and contacts
- Childhood friends
- College classmates
- Sorority sisters or fraternity brothers
- Law school classmates
- Former co-workers (nonlegal and legal)
- Neighbors
- Members of volunteer organizations to which you belong
- Former roommates
- Acquaintances from your bowling, tennis, or golf league
- Service providers (hair salon, gym, restaurant regulars)
- Doctor
- Dentist
- Spiritual leader and fellow congregants (if you belong to an organized religion)

Make a list of all of the personal contacts at your disposal. These individuals may possess important information to share with you as long as you are willing to discuss your goals and ask for help. "Stay in contact and keep in touch with your friends and colleagues … keep those networks alive," says Brian Chevlin, Deputy General Counsel, Litigation –Ice

Cream, for Unilever. "Your personal contacts are a valuable conduit in the future to find jobs."

Broaden Your Networking Circle Beyond Personal Contacts

After you have identified your personal contacts, cast an even wider net to find other networking sources. If you haven't tried to network before because you don't feel as though you have any contacts, then consider the following resources:

> Never let the fea of striking out g in your way.
>
> — BABE RUTH

Law school faculty. Many of your law professors remain active in the profession and know members of the legal community. Faculty also have access to former students who may be partners in law firms or judges. Through your faculty contacts, you can gather information by asking open-ended questions such as, "Who are the most respected litigators in town?" or "Which small firms do you think do high-quality work in the area of business and finance?" Eliciting this kind of information will help distinguish your cover letter from the rest of the pack. Instead of a letter that begins, "I am a second-year law student...," envision a cover letter that begins, "Professor Harold Smith, my family law professor, recommended that I write to you because of your reputation in the legal community and expertise in the area of divorce law...."

To enlist the help of a law professor, make an appointment during office hours to discuss your career aspirations. You don't necessarily need to be taking a professor's class in order to schedule an appointment. For instance, if you are a first-year law student who harbors an interest in intellectual property law, consider scheduling an appointment with the professor who teaches the intellectual property law survey class so that you can discuss the subjects covered in the course, career options, and related topics. This kind of information-gathering will enrich your base of knowledge and may even give you some new ideas that you had not considered before.

When meeting with a professor, bring a copy of your résumé and a list of questions. Your résumé will provide the professor with a context for your visit and help her or him understand the range of your experience to date. A list of questions will help you stay focused, particularly in the event that you become nervous. The following are some basic questions that might be appropriate to ask a professor to begin a networking conversation:

- "Professor Wright, I'm very interested in pursuing a career as a patent lawyer but I'm not sure how to go about this. I was wondering if you might be able to tell me about the various career options and whether you think I have a shot at this...."
- "Professor Jackson, thanks for meeting with me. I took your family law class because the subject is on the bar exam. But lately I've found that I really enjoy the topic and see myself practicing as a family lawyer when I graduate. I hope you might have some time to tell me about family law practice in Cleveland...."
- "I'm trying to connect with real estate lawyers in town to learn more about commercial real estate practice. Can you help me identify who the most reputable practitioners are in this area? May I use your name if I contact these individuals?"

Networking connections can also bloom in cyberspace. For example, a law student interested in space law connected with an undergraduate professor from another university via a listserv. The professor was organizing a conference on the legal and policy issues related to space law. The student volunteered to help with some of the logistics of planning the conference and, after a series of conversations, was offered the opportunity to perform some legal research for the professor that was later used in a published paper (and fulfilled the law student's writing requirement), as well as in a presentation.

Career panel discussions and speakers. Pay attention to fliers posted by your career services office advertising programs that feature speakers and panel discussions. Educational programs frequently showcase practitioners (often alumni) who are eager to speak with law students about their professional experiences and offer advice.

"Networking is consciously putting yourself in the right place at the right time," says Erin Binns, Associate Director of Career Services at Marquette University Law School in Milwaukee. "This may include attending conferences, career fairs, state bar practice session meetings, continuing legal education courses, and law school events, especially those featuring attorney/alumni presenters and panelists."

By taking the time to attend panel discussions and other informational sessions, you can hear about the latest developments and explore your compatibility with a practice area. There's little or no risk involved in making time to attend a brown bag lunch discussion about the local public defender office. You may walk away with some interesting insight or determine that this type of work is not for you. One student I know eagerly awaited the presentation by the Federal Bureau of Investigation to learn about becoming a Special Agent. (Did you know that about one-third of all Special Agents have law degrees?) The romance of being a federal agent was quickly squelched when the law student learned during the lecture that she would need to carry a gun and "shoot to kill" as part of her job duties.

In addition to providing a forum for general information-gathering, educational programs are a great way to meet lawyers informally. Typically, law students can introduce themselves to speakers following a presentation. Students who are shy about asking questions or introducing themselves at an event should send an e-mail saying thank you and initiating contact. Either way, connecting with speakers by attending educational programs is an easy way to gather information, learn, and network.

If you are an evening student who works or has other commitments during the day, don't be discouraged by the daytime scheduling of educational programs that interest you. On occasion, it might be a good investment to use personal leave or vacation time to attend a program. If your schedule prevents you from attending, take note of who the speakers are and contact them yourself by e-mail or phone. Many lawyers are listed in the Martindale-Hubbell® directory (www.martindale.com) or can be contacted through the local bar association's membership directory or by inquiring at your career services office. One of the best networking tools in the world is the personal note that says, "I'm so sorry I could not attend your presentation because I'm deeply interested in admiralty law. Would it be possible to schedule a time to meet at your convenience?"

Student bar association and other student groups. Often, student bar associations and student groups will offer educational and social programs that introduce law students to practitioners. These programs are advertised to all students and provide excellent opportunities to learn and meet lawyers. Whether you attend a "lunch-and-learn" program, a formal lecture, or a happy hour event, attendance at student bar association programs will enable you to make connections right on your own campus with participants who are friendly and receptive.

Internships and externships. Students who work as interns or externs during law school (whether for academic credit or as volunteers) have the opportunity to make important connections while gaining valuable experience. The lawyers who are supervising your work can help guide and advise you on future job searches. Use the opportunity to showcase your work ethic, explore your interest in a practice area, and leverage your work as an intern or extern to your advantage.

Mentor programs. A mentor program offers a ready-made opportunity to contact an experienced attorney who has expressed an interest in giving back by helping a student to learn more about the legal profession. Find out if either your career services office, bar association, or alumni relations office provides information about mentors. In addition to checking with your law school, investigate whether your college offers mentor programs.

When contacting a mentor, observe the basic rules of good networking etiquette that apply across the board:

- Be respectful of the mentor's time.
- Never ask for a job or demand that specific actions be taken.
- Be prepared with a copy of your résumé.

- Thank your mentor promptly.
- Follow up to update your mentor on your progress.

American Inns of Court. Investigate whether your law school offers an American Inns of Court program (www.innsofcourt.org), an excellent opportunity to meet practitioners and network. Inns of Court bring together judges, lawyers, and, in some cases, law professors and law students to study law, ethics, and professionalism on a monthly basis. Many Inns of Court are general; others focus on particular areas of practice, such as appellate litigation. Participants are divided into four categories: Masters (judges and lawyers with more than ten years of experience); Barristers (lawyers with five to ten years of experience); Associates (lawyers with less than five years of experience); and Pupils (law students).

Michelle Symank joined the Ruth Bader Ginsburg American Inn of Court at Oklahoma City University School of Law as a Pupil during her third year. Symank believes the meetings are "a great way to meet people and to talk to lawyers and judges in a relaxed atmosphere. … I feel like the members are more than willing to share any insight and wisdom with budding lawyers. And I get the impression that … they would be more than helpful in finding a job. I have found that the Inn experience is one of the best choices I've made as a law student and highly recommend it to others."

Attorney Mary Kate Coleman of Pittsburgh serves as a Master with the W. Edward Sell American Inn of Court at the University of Pittsburgh School of Law. A litigator who is also developing a mediation practice, Coleman enjoys working with law students and introducing them to the profession. "The Inn of Court is a great opportunity to get to know people and the legal community," notes Coleman. In addition to a community service project undertaken by the Inn's members, participants can take part in a mentoring program as well as a "Lunch with the Judges" event to introduce law students and practitioners to local judges.

Law school alumni functions. Alumni share a common bond and connection with you and tend to be more willing than "cold call" contacts to be of assistance. What better way to meet graduates of your law school who are receptive to offering information and advice than to attend alumni events. Visit your school's alumni office and ask if you can volunteer time to help with upcoming events such as registering guests at a party. In addition, if your school's alumni office advertises programming that is open to law students – whether a lecture series, continuing legal education program, or cocktail party – make time to attend, mix, and mingle.

Bar association membership. Bar associations offer incredible networking opportunities for law students and lawyers alike. It's worthwhile to join and participate as a student member. While offerings will vary, many bar associations offer continuing legal education programs, special speakers, networking events, and – in some cases – mentoring programs for law students. These are vehicles to connect with lawyers and expand your network beyond your law school campus.

"Get involved!" says Walter A. Wilson, III, an in-house attorney in Richmond, Virginia. "Join the local bar association, but more importantly, join the young lawyers' group of the state bar [when you graduate]. This is a great way to meet the decision-makers in the big firms and it provides you with a chance to start 'giving back' at an early age."

> may be appointed if fail, but you doomed if don't try.
>
> BEVERLY SILLS

Many state, local, and specialty bar associations offer student memberships either for free or for a nominal fee. Bar associations are typically organized by geography (state, city, county), by practice area specialties, and by affinity groups. Your career services office should have updated lists of bar associations throughout the United States. For an updated list of state, local, and specialty bar associations, see www.palidan.com/statebar.htm.

A national bar association, such as the American Bar Association, offers membership to law students and lawyers and is subdivided into sections, divisions, and forums based on practice areas. By joining the Law Student Division of the ABA (www.abanet.org/lsd), you can access many other services the American Bar Association offers, including mentor programs, writing contests, and scholarship opportunities. For a full listing of ABA sections, divisions, and forums, see www.abanet.org/sections.html to learn about networking opportunities and news about emerging areas of law.

"I encourage students to join a local bar association committee that is relevant to the field of law that they think they are interested in," says Caroline Levy, Senior Assistant Dean at Hofstra University School of Law. "Then I tell them that no one likes walking into a meeting when they don't know anyone. So, I advise that after they are on the committee, they should call the chair of the committee to introduce themselves, find out when the next committee meeting is, and express their eagerness to be an active committee member. Then, when they arrive at the meeting, they should go up to the chair and re-introduce themselves. The chair, knowing that they are a law student and a new member, will likely introduce the student to the rest of the committee."

Demetrios Eleftheriou, an associate with Willkie Farr & Gallagher LLP in Washington, D.C., encourages young lawyers interested in international law to join at least two organizations: the ABA Section on International Law and the International Association of Young Lawyers (www.aija.org). Eleftheriou also belongs to the Young Lawyers Interest Network (YIN), a new ABA committee of the Section on International Law. "The purpose of YIN is to create networking opportunities for young U.S. lawyers who are interested in international legal issues, and to help these lawyers connect with their foreign counterparts." For example, notes Eleftheriou, "YIN members seeking contacts abroad can work … to facilitate meetings with young practitioners who reside abroad."

Attend local bar association continuing legal education programs to learn about a specific field and to meet practitioners in that area. For example, if you're interested in intellectual property law, consider attending the next bar association program on developments in patent law. There may be a small fee to attend; if so, then call and ask if you can attend for a discount because you are a law student. A law student from Touro Law attended a continuing legal education class with the specific intent to meet intellectual property lawyers. She introduced herself to the person sitting next to her and started a conversation. The lawyer, it turns out, was an in-house attorney for Marvel Comics. Spurred by the meeting, the lawyer realized that Marvel could use a law clerk for the summer, and that meeting ultimately resulted in the law student being hired.

Surrender to serendipity. Serendipity plays a role in networking, so be prepared for unexpected encounters and remember, "You never know who someone knows." A law student at Temple University Beasley School of Law related this story to me: "I take the R5 commuter train to school and usually carry a textbook (or two) with me to read on the train. Frequently, a lawyer notices the title of the book and starts talking to me about his or her experiences in law school. The first lawyer who made contact with me works in-house for a large Philadelphia company. After he learned of my desire to enter the field of labor and employment law, he gave me the name of his colleague, a vice-president at his corporation who oversees the labor and employment function. I called him, we met, and he was extremely helpful. So now I carry textbooks with me whether or not I plan on reading them on the train!"

Attorney Dwayne Vance of Park City, Utah, recalled the following serendipitous encounter: "Our most recent hire was the result of an unsolicited résumé and a networking connection. My partner's mother works at a local department store in the women's department. A law student was there buying a suit for her law school graduation. As soon as my partner's mother found out why the law student was buying her outfit, she, of course, was bragging about her daughter, the attorney, up in Park City and made a connection there. Based on the chance meeting in the department store, the law student wrote to me. A job wasn't available at the time. But later on, when one became available, we went back to her and hired her."

Elaine M. Bourne of Washington University School of Law relates this story about a law student who made a networking connection while on vacation: "The law student went on a cruise and his dinner companion was a lawyer from New Jersey. As they discussed career options, the lawyer announced that her firm unfortunately did not have any openings at the time. Two weeks after the cruise, an associate at the New Jersey firm resigned suddenly and the law student received a call inquiring about his availability to interview for an entry-level position."

> "The difference between the impossible an[d] the possible li[es] in a person's determination"
> — TOMMY LASORDA

And never underestimate the power of sheer *chutzpah* to create your own serendipity. One law student who desired to work in politics in Washington, D.C., visited the city and managed to get his photo taken with Senator Bob Dole. The law student sent a copy of the photo to the senator with a note thanking him for taking the time to be photographed and mentioned his interest in politics. Senator Dole offered to meet him at some point in the future and the student followed up and received some helpful suggestions.

Internet resources. In addition to the personal contacts at your disposal, consider tapping into the vast array of opportunities on the Internet. Online sites have emerged that offer networking and job postings for members. The following are just a few of the web-based networking resources currently available:

www.careerbuilder.com is a collaboration among Gannett Co., Inc., Knight-Ridder and Tribune Company. More than 90 Gannett newspapers are now CareerBuilder.com affiliates. With a presence in over 200 local markets, CareerBuilder.com has nationwide postings.

www.classmates.com is a service of Classmates Online, Inc. Founded in 1995, this website focuses on online social networking based on listings from over 200,000 schools.

www.craigslist.org, developed by Craig Newmark, is an online community that offers a variety of opportunities to meet and network via cyberspace at no charge.

www.LinkedIn.com is a free online networking resource that enables you to tap into a network of contacts based on city and profession. Your contact information is never made public. When people contact you through LinkedIn, you can decide whether or not to accept the contact and share your contact information with them.

www.monster.com offers thousands of job postings, as well as career information and advice for free.

www.ryze.com helps people make connections and grow their networks. Basic membership is free; paid subscriptions offer advanced features. Members get a free networking-oriented home page and can send messages to other members. They can also join special Networks related to their industry, interests, or location.

www.zerodegrees.com offers a search engine that helps you capitalize on existing connections and identifies new networking contacts. You must register and complete a profile. Currently, services are free.

www.thesquare.com is the online network of alumni and students from the world's most selective colleges and universities. Founded in 1997, TheSquare was acquired in 2001 and has expanded its services to create TheSquare Network, consisting of TheSquare, SquareDating, and SquareJobs. Membership is free of charge, but only verified students and alumni of a select list of schools are eligible.

Gathering information about your current list of contacts and expanding that list to include an ever-widening circle of friends, acquaintances, and colleagues will enrich your networking potential. Your next step: Foster those connections.

MY PERSONAL NETWORK

(Use this worksheet or create your own)

FAMILY:

FRIENDS OF MY FAMILY:

COLLEGE FRIENDS:

CHILDHOOD FRIENDS:

NEIGHBORS:

CO-WORKERS (CURRENT AND FORMER):

ROOMMATES (CURRENT AND FORMER):

SORORITY OR FRATERNITY CONTACTS:

DOCTOR:

DENTIST:

HAIR SALON:

GYM:

FELLOW CONGREGANTS FROM MY CHURCH, MOSQUE, SYNAGOGUE:

Chapter 3
Socializing and Networking

Socializing can be an intimidating prospect for students and new lawyers who are not entirely comfortable attending events with strangers (and lawyers, to boot).

However, there are ways to overcome your fears and accomplish your goals. Based on my own experience, I know it's not easy to show up in an unfamiliar environment and engage in conversation with a sometimes daunting collection of individuals, many of whom know one another. Nonetheless, you, too, can learn and master the socializing skills described in this chapter.

Kevin W. Grierson, a patent attorney in Norfolk, Virginia, observes, "The best way to network is *not* to focus on networking, but to focus on *relationships*. In my experience, people will refer you to others not because you managed to stick a business card in their hand, but because they feel that they know you. … Focus on what you can do for people and how you can help them. If people you meet feel that you are genuinely concerned about their welfare and success, they will naturally want to help you be successful as well."

Thriving on the Social Circuit

The following are tips to prepare you for your next social event to maximize your networking potential.

- **Cultivate a positive mental attitude.** Successful networkers approach the process with a positive attitude, a sense of curiosity, an interest in other people, and a desire to learn more. If you are sincerely interested in making connections, then you will – eventually – "click" with others and begin to develop relationships. However, if you are merely going through the motions, socializing out of a sense of smug opportunism, or projecting negative feelings, then you will repel others and not achieve your goals.

IN THEIR OWN WORDS...

Connecting in Unlikely Places

by Jeanne M. Hammerstrom
Chief Marketing Officer, Benesch, Friedlander, Coplan & Aronoff LLP
Cleveland, Ohio

The best networkers connect people to one another and build rapport, finding out about people. Of all places — at my father's wake at a funeral home — family members were standing around greeting everyone, which is always tiring and awkward. But one person, Tom, who I always held out as the best networked attorney, visited the wake and managed to meet all five of my brothers and sisters and found something common that connected him with each of them. For instance, my brother worked at a large steel company and his co-worker was a good friend of Tom's; my sister formerly worked at Tom's old law firm; another brother had a friend in common through his work. Tom made all of my siblings feel special ... like he knew them forever, and, of all places, at a funeral home. As you might imagine, this is why he is so successful in business development for his law firm as well.

- **Create small goals.** Once you have accepted an invitation to an event, whether it is a bar association function or college reunion, set goals for yourself so you can gauge if you were successful in your networking mission. Ask yourself why you are taking the time to attend and what you seek to achieve as a result. Examples of some quantifiable goals might be:
  - o Introduce myself to three new people and learn about their work.
  - o Find out if the area of labor and employment law really interests me.
  - o Investigate if the city I want to work in following graduation is difficult for law students to break into and why.

  Consider writing down your goals before attending an event and rehearsing the questions you might ask. You may also consider conducting independent research prior to attending an event to help you become a better conversationalist. For instance, if you know you'll be attending a program featuring a prominent scholar who specializes in family law, consider researching the speaker's biography so you're familiar with his or her credentials. This can be a great conversation-starter. For example, "Did you know that Professor Jones is not only the foremost scholar in custody law in Pennsylvania but also a nationally ranked bridge player?"

- **Keep current on news and events.** In general, good networkers are naturally curious individuals who seek information and enjoy intellectual stimulation. This translates into time spent perusing newspapers, trade magazines, watching television, listening to the radio, and researching on the Internet. The best networkers are "in the know" and, as a result, everyone wants to know them.

  You don't need to become an expert in any particular area; strive to become a well-rounded individual who cultivates outside interests and enjoys a variety of activities. This may seem difficult to accomplish in law school, with the pressures of studying, tests, and job seeking; however, finding ways to balance a variety of interests will translate into a fulfilling professional and personal life, with plenty of connections.

- **Dress for success.** Dress for success by anticipating what others will be wearing at a particular event. Business attire is usually expected at professional meetings, so be prepared to wear a suit for most occasions. Pay attention to your grooming and be sure to look and feel your best. It's better to be slightly overdressed than underdressed. If you have questions about what to wear to a particular event, call ahead and ask or consult your career services office for advice.

  Nicole Tartak, a student at Fordham Law School and self-described networking maven, related the following: "I can never stress enough how important it is to dress appropriately. Believe it or not, I feel like that's half the battle. When you wear your power suit and carry yourself like a professional, you don't feel so 'student' when talking to the professionals. ... Even if it's advertised as an informal event, I still think business casual is about as casual as someone should go. The idea is that the person will look at you and say, 'I could see her fitting into the office environment.'"

- **Wearing a nametag.** Wear nametags on your right. This way, when you shake hands with someone, your name is directly in the person's line of sight. Write your name legibly and, space permitting, write the name of your school.

> "All men are caught in an inescapable network of mutuality."
>
> — MARTIN LUTHER KING,

- **Enjoy the food and drink (in moderation).** When you attend social events with a networking focus, remember that the food and drink are secondary to your primary goal: meeting and connecting with others. With that in mind, don't show up on an empty stomach; have a light snack before arriving so you're not famished. If alcohol is being served, use caution. One drink is fine, but don't overindulge because you may say and do things you'll regret later. Switch to club soda after one alcoholic beverage. And, of course, use good table manners at all times.

Balancing Act: The glass, the plate, the utensils, the handshake. Have you ever stood at a reception with a wine glass in your right hand, a canapé in your left, and — suddenly — an unfamiliar face appears and engages you in conversation? You ought to extend your hand in greeting, but you're loaded down with food and drink. What to do? Plan ahead and try to have your right hand free at all times. If you need to nibble on something before you arrive, fine. The focus of your energies ought to be on meeting and conversing, not indulging in the buffet.

- **Be aware of the impression you make.** When attending events, it's important to project a friendly, confident image.
  - o Smile.
  - o Project a positive attitude.
  - o Make eye contact.
  - o When introducing yourself, extend your hand. "Hi, my name is … and I'm a second-year law student…." Practice your professional introduction with friends and get feedback. Your handshake should be strong (neither a bone-crusher nor a limp rag).

Blogs, Websites, and Other Cyberspace Venues: Beware of the image you present online, whether you keep a blog (online journal), maintain a personal website, or engage in online discussions. Information about yourself, your political and personal views, and other data that you might prefer to keep private can be easily accessible online. Use common sense and remember that anything you write can and will be held against you.

- **Use the buddy system.** If the idea of going solo to bar association or other social programs makes you break out in hives, then find a buddy and go together. One successful "buddy system" strategy entails going to an event in a group and agreeing to split up for a half hour and meeting back at a central location. This way, you can engage individuals in conversation and then have an automatic segue to leave without monopolizing someone's time: "Excuse me, but my friends are waiting for me...."

Timothy E. Parks, Director of Business Development for the Business & Finance Practice Group at Morgan, Lewis & Bockius LLP, offers this trick to prepare you for a social event: When arriving for an event — whether it is a luncheon, continuing legal education class, or bar association gathering — ask to peruse the guest list when you register. Glance at the names of the attendees and see if you recognize any names. Having advance knowledge of the guests may help you prepare for an encounter or give you extra confidence to approach someone you know.

- When you attend your next social or professional event, remember the following acronym – **SAID** (as in "he said, she said") to ease your transition:
  - o **Survey.** Study the room and see who's there, the location of the food, drinks, and the general setup. Then enter the room, make eye contact, smile, and get something to drink or eat before you begin navigating the room.
  - o **Approach.** With a drink in hand, find a friendly face and approach a group to enter the conversation. A good general rule is to try and break into conversations with three or more people in a group. When you see two people engaged in a conversation, they may be having a private talk and would prefer not to be

disturbed. But a group of three or more is more likely to be engaged in general social banter and would welcome a newcomer.

- o **Introduce.** Stand at the periphery of the circle, smile, make eye contact and then, when someone gives you a nod or smile, it's your opportunity to step into the circle and introduce yourself.
- o **Depart.** Don't overstay your welcome by remaining long after the conversation loses steam. Use the "Conversation Enders" (discussed on page 46) to extricate yourself from the conversation and move on to your next encounter.

■ **Carry business cards.** Some law students carry business cards with their relevant contact information. You can purchase inexpensive business cards with your name, e-mail address, telephone number, your school, and year of graduation professionally printed. Thus, when a lawyer extends a business card for further contact, you can do the same. Many law students find exchanging cards to be an effective, professional way to interact and better than jotting contact information on a cocktail napkin. Some law school career services offices encourage law students to create business cards and assist with the production. For instance, at Washington and Lee University School of Law, students can create their own business cards using a template created by the Career Planning and Professional Development Office. The cards display the logo of the law school and the student's name and contact details, as well as his or her year of expected graduation.

If you decide to carry and exchange business cards with potential contacts, remember that the burden of following up and keeping in contact lies with you, the law student. Don't assume that handing a business card to a contact relieves you of the duty to follow up. The ball is squarely in your court at all times.

Business Card Etiquette

Have you ever been carded at a social event? I'm not referring to a request for identification at the bar. Some less sophisticated souls believe that networking consists of tossing business cards at passersby and then running out of the room. I once attended a women's networking event where one participant literally walked from table to table and practically threw her business cards in the middle of each table, smiled, and walked on to the next group. Was she effective? No, because she did not understand the etiquette of furnishing a business card.

First, bring business cards with you to any event where you may meet someone. This means stashing business cards in your wallet, purse, car, briefcase, and suit pocket. Never go anywhere without your business card.

A business card should be presented to someone *after* you have spent at least five minutes in conversation. The business card is your chance to further the connection and exchange contact information. For example, "It's been a pleasure chatting. I'd love to continue the conversation and tell you the author of that book on Italian cuisine. Here's my card; let's stay in touch." Typically, the recipient will then reciprocate with a business card.

When you are handed a business card, take a moment and examine the card, the person's title, company, and general presentation, and then put it away. If appropriate, offer a compliment to show appropriate respect for the person furnishing the card: "That's a great design; very eye-catching."

When attending a conference or meeting where you might collect many business cards, one trick to keep information straight is to jot down on the back of each business card some pertinent information or words to spark your memory about that person. Merely collecting business cards will not make you more connected. You will need to follow up and continue the connection.

Many networking experts talk about business card management systems. My personal system involves entering the information into my PalmPilot® with as much information as possible to spur my memory. I add to this information over time, cull my files on an annual basis, and generally keep tabs on my progress and ever-widening circle of contacts.

A Crash Course in Conversation Skills

Successful networkers know how to ask questions and engage in conversations. Cultivate careful listening skills, be mindful of the conversational flow, and remember that you're there to learn and gain advice. In the words of Susan and Larry Terkel, authors of *Small Change* (Tarcher, 2004), "Employ the Golden Rule of Listening: Listen as you would have others listen to you."

"Be a sponge with elephant ears," suggests veteran career coach Judy Rosemarin. "Your job is to absorb information and become self-informed. The best networkers are open and curious people."

The Three S's of Conversations

Smile. People who smile and appear at ease will always attract people. Don't be afraid to smile, make eye contact, and signal that you want to interact socially.

Shake hands. In business situations, it's always expected that you will introduce yourself and shake hands in greeting. Have your hand free and ready to extend in a professional handshake.

Salutation. While shaking hands, be ready to introduce yourself briefly. "Hello, I'm _____ and I'm in my third year at _____ Law School."

When conversing, always listen attentively, acknowledge, and then articulate your professional goals at the appropriate interval. The following are some sample questions to pose:

- "I'm a second-year student, so right now my focus is on finding a job with a firm in Tulsa this summer. Before law school, I clerked for a small firm and now I want to explore a larger office environment. Do you know about larger firms in Tulsa?"
- "I'd like to find a part-time job this semester with a firm that works on plaintiffs' medical malpractice cases. I worked as a registered

nurse before law school and understand the medical issues, so it's a natural fit for me. Who are the most reputable malpractice lawyers in town?"

- "Are there entertainment lawyers in St. Louis? I heard that you have to work in either Los Angeles or New York if you want to do that kind of work. Is that true?"
- "Tell me about your work. ... That sounds interesting. Do you like what you do?"

Don't be afraid to tell people what you're seeking. Since few of us are mind readers (I'm certainly not), you need to tell people what you need. Simply put: Ask. "Do you know who the best divorce mediators are in San Francisco?" "Can you tell me how to identify the top labor law firms in the region?" "How can I learn more about nonprofit management opportunities in Chicago?" Posing direct questions to potential sources will help lead you to the resources you seek.

Tackling "Table Talk" Programs

Most law schools' career services offices offer large-scale networking programs at least once a year. These events typically entail a room full of lawyers, usually arranged by practice area, with the chance for law students to mingle informally and ask questions of practitioners.

If you're inclined to skip a program of this nature, reconsider. It's a great way to become a more confident networker and practice your skills with the support of your career services office. Remember that most participants will be alumni and, thus, already predisposed to have a connection to you and a desire to help share information.

Matthew L. Pascocello of the Office of Career Services at American University Washington College of Law (WCL) has produced a student networking event called "WCL Connects" where representatives from area trade and professional associations, including bar associations, were invited to interact with students in order to share information about how law students can become more involved and visible among practitioners in their selected fields of interest. "Invariably, students walk away from this event with leads about internships, invitations to attend upcoming programs, and information about membership, scholarship, and writing opportunities, to say nothing of the tremendous contacts they make with well-connected professionals who have a real interest in helping students with their professional development," notes Pascocello.

Many law schools prepare law students for "Table Talk" style networking events by creating advance programming to help students feel comfortable and acquire useful networking skills. For example, in preparation for American University's WCL Connects program, and also as an independent networking "how to" session, the career services office offers a program entitled "The Art of Networking Session." Pascocello explains that this session is the place where students learn real strategies about how to maximize the WCL Connects program, as well as other related networking opportunities, such as informational interviews, career fairs, receptions, and chance encounters.

"In addition to creating significant hand-out materials, including mock e-mails for situation-driven requests for informational interviews, the Art of Networking program offered students the opportunity to engage in role play as well as the chance to craft and practice their 30-second pitch," Pascocello recounts. Can't attend the training program? American University, along with an increasing number of law schools, offers podcasts of their programs, complete with an online resource center where students can download corresponding handouts and materials.

The following are some tips to help you tackle your next "Table Talk" event:

- Dress in business casual attire. No need to wear a suit and tie, but opt for a professional look rather than gym clothes.
- Bring your résumé, but do not offer it unless requested. Sometimes conversations take a very interesting turn and a lawyer will ask to see your credentials. Be prepared.

- Come with some basic questions to ask and a brief introduction:

  > "Hi, my name is ____ and I'm a second-year student. I'm interested to hear what your work entails at the Department of Justice. I've always been interested in working as a federal prosecutor."

- Circulate to a few tables and don't monopolize anyone's time.
- Follow up. If you connected with a lawyer and enjoyed learning about his or her work, don't be shy about writing a short e-mail or written thank you note to say how much you appreciated the event.

Secrets of Good Conversation from the Experts

"Remember that good conversation is not a monologue (you doing all the talking or the other person doing all the talking) but a give and take," write Susan and Larry Terkel, authors of *Small Change*. "Aim for balance, aspire for interesting. Don't expect small talk and casual conversation to reach the heights of a seminar in philosophy. If you rely on the word ask, you will always be able to keep the conversation going — or have a reasonable excuse to get going."

One career services professional uses a beach ball metaphor to describe a good conversation: Think of passing the conversational ball between individuals, never hogging the ball or failing to pass it along to the next person. Conversation is a give-and-take, where you need to listen, respond, and keep the ball in motion.

Susan RoAne, networking expert and author of *What Do I Say Next? Talking Your Way to Business and Social Success*, offers this piece of advice: Good conversationalists conduct themselves like the hosts (even if they are the guests). "Hosts are interested in other people's comfort, and go out of their way to mix, mingle, and connect people. They greet others, make them feel welcome, introduce them to others, share stories, ask questions, and listen to the responses. Hosts cheerfully and politely excuse themselves once the new kid is settled into a conversation."

Conversation Starters

The best minglers have an innate interest in other people and are eager to learn about and connect with others. I find that, in a business networking context, it's always appropriate to ask about a person's work or his or her motivation for engaging in a certain field of practice, or to share a sincere compliment or observations about the event itself (location, turnout, decor). Here are some examples of good conversations starters:

- "Hi, my name is ______ and I'm a law student at ______" (shake hands).
- "What a great get-together! I never knew the museum offered their exhibit halls for public events. What do you think of the exhibit?"
- "You're from Chicago? That's a great city. I have some friends from college who are living and working in Evanston. I love visiting there."
- "What motivated you to become a district attorney? I hear it's a very competitive process."
- "Are you a member of the Young Lawyers Division? What activities do they have planned for this year?"
- "How about those Red Sox...."

Conversation Enders

All good things, including conversations, must come to an end. The following are some suggested segues to help you transition out of a conversation. You don't want to turn on your heel and leave abruptly. Instead, try these lines to graciously move on:

- "It's been a pleasure speaking with you, Jill. I promised Reid I'd say hello and I want to catch him before he leaves." (shake hands).
- "Nice chatting with you, Frank. I'm going to get something to drink now. Let's keep in touch." (shake hands).
- "A pleasure to meet you, Marcia. I hope our paths cross again. If you'll excuse me...." (shake hands).

IN THEIR OWN WORDS...

Tips for Starting and Ending Conversations

by Debra Fine

Author of *The Fine Art of Small Talk (Hyperion, 2005) (www.debrafine.com)*

1. Come up with three things to talk about when preparing for a function, along with a couple generic questions that will get others talking. If you've met the client before, remind yourself of things about her, such as a vacation she was headed to or specifics about her family.
2. Be the first to say "hello." If you're not sure the other person will remember you, give the gift of your name to help out. For example, "Jared Holst? Debra Fine ... good to see you again." Smile first and always shake hands when you meet someone.
3. Take your time during introductions. Make an extra effort to remember names and use them frequently. Exhibit host behavior by introducing others who join the group to each other.
4. Get another person talking by leading with a common ground statement regarding the occasion or location and then asking a related open-ended question. For example, "What do you hope to gain from this conference?" or "What have you heard about the speakers?" You can also ask them about their trip in or how they know the guests of honor.
5. Show interest in your conversational partner by actively listening and giving verbal feedback. Maintain eye contact. Never glance around the room while they are talking to you.
6. Listen more than you talk.
7. Be prepared to have something interesting to contribute. Staying on top of current events will provide you with great conversation builders, leading with: "What do you think of ... ?" "Have you heard ... ?" "What is your take on ... ?" Spare us from your opinion unless you remember to follow up with "What is your opinion?" or "Tell me your thoughts on ..."
8. Be aware of your body language. People who look or act ill at ease make others uncomfortable. Act confident and comfortable even when you're not.
9. Have a few exit lines ready, so that you can both gracefully move on. For example, "I need to check in with a client over there," "I skipped lunch today, so I need to visit the buffet," or "Who do you know at this meeting who could help me with ... ?"

Conversation Killers

Some conversation topics are explicitly off limits and these subjects include:

- **Politics.** Engaging in conversations about another person's political views is a no-win, particularly if you're trying to make new networking contacts. Steer clear of making your political views known and demeaning those who disagree with your views. The exception to this rule is that if you're attending a political fund-raising event and you know everyone in the room holds similar viewpoints, then a discussion about politics is appropriate.
- **Health-related issues, including pregnancy.** Avoid discussions about health, illness, and – of course – never assume a woman is pregnant unless she tells you her due date or is actually in labor before your very eyes.
- **Money, including salary.** Discussion about money (how much a car or house costs, the cost of your last vacation, salary) steps over polite boundaries and the other person may not feel comfortable sharing information with a stranger.
- **Religion.** Even if you're simply curious, don't quiz people about their religious beliefs unless this information is volunteered in some context. You never want to ask people point-blank: "Are you a Mormon?" However, if in the course of the conversation, an individual volunteers that they just returned from a church mission to Haiti, you can feel comfortable following up with questions about the type of church, the nature of the mission, and the like.
- **Age.** Questions or observations about age should be avoided.

Networking to Fit Your Style

Networking need not consist of raucous socializing, back slapping, popularity contests, or any of the other negative images that may come to mind. While socializing will help connect you to others, there are quieter alternatives for those who are less gregariously inclined.

If you tend to be shy, dislike large social events, or find meeting strangers to be stressful, consider the following strategies and ideas to take the pain out of parties and other large gatherings:

- **Know about the event and plan accordingly.** If you are attending a reception that precedes an awards ceremony, don't feel obligated to show up at the precise starting time and languish. Many social event starting times assume that the party does not get into full swing until 15 to 30 minutes following the official start time. With that in mind, show up when the party is well along and you won't feel uncomfortable waiting for the event to begin. In addition, if you know there's a cocktail hour either before or after the main event, plan accordingly when making your entrance and exit.
- **Bring a posse.** Utilize the "buddy system" mentioned earlier when attending large events. Bring a friend (or several friends) and agree to socialize together. If you arrive together, make a plan to split up for 20 minutes, engage others, then reconvene at a mutually agreed upon time. Having a buddy (or buddies) at the event will give you an automatic out if you're trapped in a dead-end conversation or feel uncomfortable.
- **Let people know.** If you're nervous about showing up at an event and feel like an outsider, consider calling the event chair in advance or telling the person at the registration table about your situation. Sometimes, the honesty of saying, "I'm just a second-year law student and I'm sort of intimidated by all this...." will open the door to having someone say, "Let me introduce you to some of my colleagues."
- **Carve out a corner at a large function.** If you are attending a large function and feel daunted at the thought of navigating a ballroom, survey the room when you enter and find an area to claim as your "home base." Don't feel obligated to move from group to group interjecting yourself into conversations. Either sit at a table or park yourself near the appetizers and let the people come to you.
- **Gravitate toward smaller events or one-on-one meetings.** There is no commandment that requires anyone to attend large-scale networking events. If crowds truly overwhelm you and you don't have a circle of friends or classmates to help you navigate the process,

then focus on smaller get-togethers and one-on-one meetings. You can make great connections in small venues as effectively as in larger ones. And – who knows? – with time and experience, you may find that big events are not as scary as you once thought.

- **Give yourself a time limit.** While veteran party-goers might stay for the entire event, give yourself a time limit and have somewhere else to go. If you give yourself parameters (for example, "I can stay for one hour and then I have to get back and finish my reading for tomorrow") you will view the event as having a clear beginning, middle, and end and you'll make better use of your time.
- **Be an attentive listener.** The best networkers engage in attentive, active listening. You need not be chatty, a natural comic, or anything other than yourself in order to listen well and engage in a conversation.
- **Read all about it.** You can learn to become a better networker and enjoy social events more through practice and study. There are many good resources available, including *What Do I Say Next? Talking Your Way to Business and Social Success* by Susan RoAne. Her practical advice and insights will teach you new skills and impart confidence in social settings.

The Party's Over: Making the Individual Approach

Large events can be a great way to meet a variety of people at one time. However, many valuable networking contacts are forged through independent research or individual referrals. When someone offers you the name of a contact and gives permission to use his or her name as the source of the recommendation, initiate contact while the lead is fresh. If you're unsure about the next step, simply ask the person offering you information: "What should my next step be?"

Follow through on the information you are given. Getting a lead will prove useless unless you act on the information you are given. The following are suggestions for taking concrete steps to connect:

- **Write it down.** Carry a small pad and pen to jot down names and contact information. During the course of casual conversation, it's easy to forget information (was it John Smith or Jan Schmidt?), and once you walk away, it's difficult to reconstruct the facts. If someone offers you information, then take a moment and write it down.
- **Always ask if you can use someone's name.** Sometimes information will be offered in a general sense and the person offering the information will not want their name used in connection with the contact. Be sensitive to the fact that you should not use people's names without their specific permission. Simply ask, "May I mention your name if I contact Fred Jackson about his international tax practice?" Your contact will give you a simple "yes" or "no" and you must honor their request.
- **Apprise your contact of your progress.** When you proceed to act on the information you are given, be sure to reconnect with your contact, thank them for the information, and let them know the steps you have taken. A short e-mail or handwritten thank you note will help them to keep you in mind for future contacts. If appropriate, you can include a copy of your résumé for ease of reference.

Here is an example of what you might write to apprise a contact of your progress:

Dear Elizabeth,

Thank you so much for suggesting that I contact Marc Morrison about small firm practice in Detroit. We met yesterday at his office and he had many good ideas about contacts and job search strategies. Thank you again for being so kind about referring me to Marc. I feel confident that I am making inroads to finding a great job when I graduate in May. I will update you from time to time on my progress and hope our paths cross again soon at another alumni event.

With best wishes,

Donna

- **Keep records of your networking activities.** You can track your performance and conduct effective follow-up if you maintain your networking information in one place. Important information to keep includes the name of the person you met, their title, employer, where you met, and the information you were given. A sample networking log page can be found at the end of this chapter.

  It can also be helpful to jot down some identifying information about each person to help spur your memory in the future. For instance, if you met a knowledgeable person on the topic of entertainment law and you had a good discussion about her recent visit to the Alps, then jot down something to spur your recollection ("hiked in the Alps to celebrate her fortieth birthday").

  Whether you keep your records in a notebook, Filofax®, PalmPilot® or other database system, review and refresh your information over time and track your progress. You will find that your connections begin to intertwine and that as you develop your web of contacts, cultivation will become easier if you keep accurate records.

Generally, sending a typed letter by first-class mail is the most common way to initiate contact. Use a regular business envelope and tri-fold your letter. If you decide to send an e-mail, make sure the subject line is clear and unambiguous. Avoid generalities, such as "Meeting you" or "Help." Instead, use your contact's name to get the attention of the recipient. For instance: "Jason Philips – Referral."

With all correspondence, be direct, polite, and **never, ever ask for a job**. An approach letter should include the following information:

- Who referred you to the person you're addressing
- Why you picked this person to speak with and how you hope he or she can help you
- Who you are
- Your current status
- The specific information you are seeking
- How much time you need

- When you will call to schedule an appointment

The following is an example of an approach letter:

Dear Ms. Jackson,

Jason Philips suggested that I contact you for advice regarding the names of family law practitioners in St. Louis. Jason was singing your praises at a bar association event where we met and encouraged me to contact you for advice.

I am currently a third-year law student at Boston University School of Law and will graduate in May. While I grew up in St. Louis and intend to return home to take the bar exam and practice law, I have lived in Boston for the past six years and have not cultivated my hometown contacts. Throughout law school I have focused on trial advocacy and family law matters. I received an "A" in Family Law, taught by Professor Martin, and spent the past summer clerking for a judge in the local family court. I enclose a copy of my résumé for your review and suggestions.

I would truly appreciate the opportunity to meet you and learn more about the family law practitioners in St. Louis. During Thanksgiving vacation, I plan to be in St. Louis visiting family and would be grateful for the opportunity to meet you at your convenience. I will call next week to see if you are amenable to meeting with me. In addition, you can reach me either by e-mail or telephone.

Thank you in advance for your time and consideration. I look forward to meeting you and learning more about your work.

Sincerely,

Jan Jones

Telephone Etiquette

Telephone calls can be tricky and may put a prospective networking contact in the uncomfortable position of responding right away without thinking about options or — worse still — commence a game of phone tag that can become annoying. If you must telephone a potential networking contact, employ the following tips to ensure a productive conversation:

- Relax. Take a few deep breathes before dialing the number. You want to sound natural and relaxed; loud enough to be heard, but not too loud. And remember not to speak too fast.
- Identify yourself. Be sure to give your first and last name. If you were referred, give the name of the referral source.
- State the purpose of your call.
- Be prepared. Jot down questions before you pick up the receiver. Some law students even script their entire introduction and type it double-spaced on a sheet of paper.
- Determine the next step. If you are trying to schedule a meeting, make sure you make the "ask" and get an answer.
- Thank the person for his or her time and assistance both at the end of the conversation and in writing, if appropriate.

Successful Meeting Tips

While many networking exchanges are initiated via letter, e-mail, or telephone, some of the best opportunities arise when you meet face to face. When you schedule a networking meeting, remember that the person who has generously agreed to spend time with you is offering their advice and insight. Their time is precious and you need to treat them with deference, respect, and gratitude. Adhere to the following tips to make your next networking meeting a success:

- **Defer to the convenience of the person offering the advice.** Set the right tone by being deferential about the time and place of the meeting. Don't dictate the terms of where and when; be polite.
- **Be time-sensitive.** Respect the time of the person with whom you are meeting. Arrive on time. Don't monopolize another's time or overstay your welcome. Generally, meetings over coffee ought to take no more than 30 minutes and lunch-time meetings should not exceed one hour.

- **Come prepared.** Do your research and be prepared with some questions. Have paper and pen at the ready to jot down information.
- **Say thank you.** Write a thank you letter promptly.
- **Follow up.** Log your contact's name in your networking records and engage in follow-up.

Picking Up the Check: Who Pays the Tab?

When the time comes to pick up the tab, remember that the person receiving advice ought to be prepared to pay. After all, the person who agreed to meet you is taking the time and offering the knowledge; your responsibility is to pay for that time. Meeting at the contact's office or for coffee is probably the most cost-effective route, but if you meet for lunch or dinner, be prepared to foot the bill. Of course, in some cases, a particularly kind and generous individual will offer to pay or split the tab, but you cannot depend on the generosity of others, so be prepared to pay.

The only exception to this rule: If you are invited to a private club, then the person inviting you will pick up the tab.

Dealing with Rejection ... or When to Call It Quits

After making contacts and trying to schedule meetings either via phone, e-mail, or letter, when is it time to call it quits? You will, no doubt, experience varying degrees of success as you attempt to connect with others. Some individuals will respond to you immediately and enthusiastically. Others will lag in their responses and need to be prompted gently. Still others will ignore you completely.

Rejection is part and parcel of the networking (and job search) process. You should expect that some contacts will result in great leads and ideas; other contacts will fall flat. Whether this is due to busy schedules, deadlines, family distractions, personality conflicts, or other factors is moot. Rather than try to analyze what went wrong, decide that after three polite attempts you will move on and explore other networking contacts.

This means that, if you initiate contact with a networking source with a friendly e-mail, letter, or phone call, followed by a follow-up e-mail or phone call three to five business days later, and then one last e-mail to no avail, then move on and don't dwell on it. Making repeated attempts to get a response will only distract you from your ultimate goal and annoy the other person. See the world as a nearly endless array of possible contacts in which this one contact did not pan out. Hold no grudges and simply proceed to the next opportunity. Besides, your paths may cross again.

IN THEIR OWN WORDS...

Showing Up

by Deborah Schneider
Co-author, *Should You Really Be A Lawyer? The Guide to Smart Career Choices Before, During and After Law School* (DecisionBooks, 2004) (www.shouldyoureally.com)

Woody Allen has said, famously, that "Eighty percent of success in life is just showing up."

This is most definitely true when it comes to your job search: Showing up can go a long way toward helping you land a job.

By "showing up," I mean attending events where you'll meet lawyers and others who can help you with your job search.

What types of events should you attend? For starters, go to legal events sponsored by your local bar association, such as continuing legal education programs (CLEs), brown bag lunches, social events (some bar associations have book clubs), speakers' series, and the like. In addition, attend events sponsored by any law-related organization in your community, organizations for women lawyers, plaintiffs' lawyers, employment lawyers, criminal lawyers, or any other group of lawyers whose work interests you. Showing up to these types of events is especially valuable for busy law students because it's an efficient way to meet many lawyers all at once and because attorneys tend to admire students who take the initiative to be there.

Each year, savvy law students get jobs just because they showed up at an event and hit off with someone they met there. Catherine, a recent law school grad who was looking for a public interest legal job, was one of them. Determined to improve her networking efforts, she checked her local bar association's website and discovered an upcoming panel discussion about public interest law. She made it to the event, chatted with plenty of the public interest lawyers there, and even stood up and asked the panelists a question related to their remarks. (She also managed to work in that she was looking for a public interest job.) *[continued]*

IN THEIR OWN WORDS... CONTINUED

After the panel, five — yes, five — local attorneys approached her and offered to help her with her job search. Three of them even invited her to interview with their organizations. She followed up with them all and ultimately accepted a job with one. And all because she made an effort to show up!

By the way, I practice what I preach — showing up is how I've gotten nearly every job I've ever held. I landed three of my last four positions because I met someone at a dinner, a luncheon, and a happy hour (respectively). What does that leave? Breakfast! I don't know what my next job will be, but I'm pretty sure that I'll get it as a result of showing up at a breakfast.

SAMPLE NETWORKING LOG

Name ____

Address ____

City ____________________ State ____________ Zip ______________

Telephone ____

Fax ____

E-mail ____

Employer ____

Where you met ____

Contacts made _______________________________________

Follow-up history _____________________________________

____

____

____

____

Chapter 4

Informational Interviewing

Networking can assume many forms, ranging from social events to the prearranged meeting to the serendipitous encounter. By becoming more mindful of the opportunities at your disposal, you can continually expand your circle of contacts. One such opportunity is the "informational interview," which can be defined broadly as a meeting, arranged in advance, to obtain advice from an experienced professional about a specific career path to enhance one's professional development and job seeking skills.

This chapter will teach you everything you need to know about informational interviews. Informational interviews offer yet another way for you to connect to others, learn about career options, and expand your base of knowledge. The more knowledgeable you become, the better equipped you will be to create meaningful connections.

What Is Informational Interviewing?

Think of informational interviewing as a specialized form of networking in which you speak informally with a professional in a practice area or career niche of interest to you. "Informational interviewing is a way of conducting career research," says Judy Rosemarin, founder and president of Sense-Able Strategies, Inc., a New York-based career coaching firm. "You need to survey others and get information so you can make an informed decision."

"Law students often complain that informational interviews don't feel like a concrete job search activity, such as sending résumés and applying to online job listings," relates author and attorney Deborah Schneider. "However, law students need to realize that informational interviews are one of the most valuable ways they can use their time and that they are doing something concrete: They are building relationships. And relationships are the key to getting hired."

— SIR FRANCIS BACON

Informational interviews enable you to:

- Learn in-depth about a specific job or career path;
- Gain an understanding of current career developments;
- Get information about what opportunities may arise in a given practice area or organization;
- Learn about jobs and legal career paths you did not know existed;
- Help you decide what type of job or career path is right for you;
- Gain information about nontraditional legal careers;
- Practice promoting your skills and accomplishments in a non-pressured environment; and
- Cultivate a network of people who may be helpful to you throughout your career.

In short, the purpose of an informational interview is to gather information and cultivate contacts, not to interview for a specific position or ask for a job.

Mark Dighton, Director of School Relations for the Practising Law Institute in New York, observes that informational interviewing can create an effective referral system to expand one's network of contacts and provide information about jobs as well. "It is often the case that you'll be put in contact with other people who may know of jobs, or may even have jobs," say Dighton. "With a reference from an informational interview, you've got a foot in the door, you know someone in common, and that can make all the difference. This has worked for me several times. I've gone for informational interviews at places where I knew they didn't have jobs but learned that they could put me in touch with people who did."

As do so many students, I attended law school with a vague notion that unlimited possibilities abounded for smart, hard-working individuals with law degrees. I wasn't quite sure what all of the possibilities entailed, but I felt confident that doors would open for me. While this proved to be true in the long run, I wish I had been more courageous during law school about asking career-related questions, demanding answers, and putting my theories (which were sometimes far off base) to the test. Imagine the time I could have saved, the false starts I could have averted, and the dead ends I could have avoided if I had not been timid about asking others for advice.

Scheduling informational interviews would have saved me so much time and aggravation; yet I was shy and nervous about demonstrating my lack of knowledge. Law school inculcates the notion that you should always have the answer, no matter what. The Socratic Method discourages law students who appear naive or inexperienced, and this aversion to revealing weakness carries over into our career choices.

Law students, whose only legal experience thus far is through classes and perhaps through limited work experience, are left to wonder what a particular career path might be like. While researching career paths through books, magazines, and websites can be very helpful, there is no substitute for actually getting out and asking questions from an expert, someone who is doing the kind of work you think you want to pursue someday.

Informational interviewing allows you to ask questions, probe for answers, and discover for yourself if a particular path is right for you, all without committing emotional capital to the need to find the "right" position from the start. Making contacts through informational interviewing will also enable you to broaden your circle of contacts and increase the chances that you'll "click" with another person who could have a profound influence on your life.

Don't be nervous about appearing unknowledgeable or uncertain. As in all networking activities, you need to proceed with a sense of curiosity, a feeling of gratitude, and a sincere desire to learn and grow as a professional. Those who offer their expertise generally do so with great generosity of heart. Follow these guidelines and you'll find that informational interviewing will enrich your networking circle.

Getting Started

> If you have knowledge, let others light their candles at it.
>
> — MARGARET FULLER

Begin by framing your career search issue. What are you seeking to learn? (By the way, the answer is not how to get a job. Informational interviewing is strictly about data gathering, not job seeking.) For every law student, this issue will be different. Think about what interests you, what geographic areas are your top priorities, and any other short- and long-range career plans you may be considering. Write down the issues that you would like to learn more about through an informational interview. For example: "I want to find out if nonprofit organizations typically hire full-time lawyers and, if so, what the career path looks like," or "Are there any lawyers who are certified as divorce mediators and is this a growing field?"

Dream big at this stage and don't be afraid to frame the issue. By articulating what you're seeking to acquire, you can then focus on the next step: finding people with whom to speak.

In order to arrange an informational interview, begin by identifying people you already know with information or contacts that may be useful to you. Refer to the end of chapter 2 for a list of familiar individuals already in your circle who might be knowledgeable or know someone who can help you with your particular issue.

Next, create a list of people you would like to meet but do not yet know. This is your chance to be truly creative and daring. Think of people – famous, living on another continent, whatever your heart desires – who could provide you with meaningful career-related information. For instance, if you're interested in:

- Becoming a legal news commentator – you may want to interview the local media legal expert.
- Running a local political campaign – you may want to learn about lawyers who have entered politics, perhaps the mayor of your town or another prominent local official involved in party politics.
- Practicing plaintiffs' medical malpractice law – you probably want to meet the lawyer in town who has secured the largest jury award this year.
- Teaching law at a university or college someday – consider speaking with a full-time or adjunct professor about his or her career path.

Identifying More Sources

> ur knowledge is e amassed ought and ‹perience of numerable inds.
>
> – RALPH WALDO EMERSON

To identify sources beyond your familiar circle of contacts, you will need to conduct some research. Your mother might know the name of the best tax attorney in Philadelphia, but what if you want to talk to a music industry executive about legal jobs in Los Angeles?

Here are some ideas for identifying informational interview sources:

- **Career services office.** The professionals in your career services office have access to alumni, colleagues, friends, and others who could assist you. Schedule an appointment with your career services office and explain your desire to conduct informational interviews on a particular subject. The contact information you want may be closer than you think. In addition, educational programs that showcase alumni offer law students a great opportunity to ask questions and arrange for a more in-depth informational interview opportunity. Did you enjoy hearing about the lawyer who works for the National Labor Relations Board and would you now like to sit down and ask her more questions? There is nothing stopping you from making a request for an informational interview.

- **Law school faculty.** Talk to your law school professors and see if they might know individuals who can help answer your questions through informational interviews. Schedule an appointment, explain your interests, and see if a law professor who practices in a similar area might be able to refer you to a colleague.
- **Law school alumni mentor programs.** Many law schools offer mentor programs, either through the alumni relations office or career services office. Mentors are typically graduates who have volunteered to talk to law students about their career paths. Ask if your law school offers a mentor program and determine the steps necessary to access the information and make contacts.
- **College or graduate school mentor programs.** As with your law school, check whether or not your college or former graduate school offers a mentor program and inquire about the steps necessary to participate.
- **Bar association mentor programs.** Many bar associations offer mentor programs to members. By becoming a law student member, you can access mentors and arrange informational interviews.
- **Martindale-Hubbell on LexisNexis®** enables law students to research lawyers listed in the directory by practice area, law school, year of graduation, college, city, and state, as well as by place of birth and foreign languages spoken (if listed). These are all data points for law students to pinpoint practitioners who may fit their profile.
- **Newspaper and magazine articles.** Have you ever read a fascinating magazine article about an individual and thought to yourself, "I'd love to learn more about how she managed to start a successful catering business after working as a lawyer for ten years!" There is absolutely nothing stopping you from contacting the individual in question and requesting his or her time to learn more. Don't be afraid to ask. What's the worst that can happen? You may be told "no" or you might be ignored. So what! Move on and find your next informational interview source.

- **Networking events and other public forums.** I recently attended a women's networking event where the keynote speaker was a local real estate developer. The real estate developer was getting lots of local media coverage for her innovative way of reclaiming old buildings and converting them into residential space. As I sat in the audience I thought she would be a terrific speaker for a nonprofit group for which I volunteer. Her energy, intelligence, and business acumen were inspiring. I e-mailed her a note the next day and introduced myself. The result: the real estate developer graciously agreed to address our group later that year. I simply asked.
- **Internet research.** Explore websites that offer networking opportunities. For a list of suggested Internet-based networking sites, see chapter 2. In addition, if you the know the names of particular individuals you would like to meet, consider using an Internet search engine such as Google® to find contact information.

Making the Approach

Once you have identified a potential contact, write to inquire about the possibility of scheduling an interview time. The approach letter can be sent either as e-mail (in the body of the e-mail because attachments may be difficult to open or deleted as spam) or via first-class mail in a business envelope. Telephoning is inadvisable because the information you seek to convey about yourself and the request you are making are not conducive to the immediacy of the telephone. The timing of an e-mail message or letter better enables the recipient to consider your request and respond accordingly.

Begin by introducing yourself briefly and explaining the purpose of your letter. If a mutual acquaintance, colleague, or law school faculty or staff member recommended the contact, then you should always begin your correspondence with that information. Similarly, if you read about the individual in a newspaper article, be sure to reference that as well. I recommend a prominent "Re:" line before the salutation stating "Request for informational interview" or similar words to distinguish your letter from unsolicited cover letters and résumés seeking jobs.

The following is an example of correspondence requesting an informational interview:

Your name
Street address
City, State, Zip
Date

Recipient's name
Street address
City, State, Zip

Re: Request for informational interview

Dear ___________:

Professor Elliott Ness suggested that I contact you to arrange an informational interview because of my strong interest in pursuing a career in criminal defense law. As a first-year law student at ______________, I am currently taking Criminal Law and Criminal Procedure. Both courses have sparked a strong interest in criminal defense work, but I am wary about making a decision without further investigation.

Professor Ness wisely suggested that I speak to an experienced professional who might be able to shed light on the career options that may be available, as well as suggesting summer work experience and post-graduate experience that would be viewed favorably by a future employer. I am also interested in learning about the day-to-day challenges you face as a criminal defense lawyer. This is not a request for a job; my desire to speak with you stems from my strong desire to gather information and develop a network of contacts who may be able to supply me with first-hand information to help me make informed career decisions.

I would be grateful for any time you might be able to spare to speak with me. I can visit your office at your convenience and promise to be brief and direct. Your advice would be invaluable to me as I explore career options and learn more about criminal defense work in _______.

I can be reached at (123) 456-7891 or via e-mail at ______. Thank you in advance for your time and I look forward to hearing from you soon.

Sincerely,
<signature>
Your name

Here is an example of an approach letter as an e-mail message:

To: Recipient's name

From: Your name

Subject: Request for informational interview (Name of referral in parentheses, if appropriate)

Dear ___________,

I read the article in The Jasper Chronicle about your work as one of the few real estate lawyers in the U.S. who specializes in oil and gas law. As a second-year law student at _________, I read the article with great interest because I want to work in real estate law and finance work following graduation. In particular, I am interested in learning about trends in real estate practice in Wyoming, the most sought-after classes or skills that future employers might focus upon, and the challenges of practicing real estate law in the Western U.S.

I would appreciate the chance to meet with you when I visit my family for Thanksgiving vacation or via telephone or e-mail at your convenience. Thank you in advance and good luck with your practice.

Sincerely,

Your name
E-mail
Phone number

Prepare for Your Informational Interview

Create a list of questions you intend to ask at the interview. Since you have initiated contact and are conducting the interview, you must be prepared.

Research the individual's career and his or her firm, agency, or organization. You can conduct basic research on the Internet using Google or another search engine. Peruse the firm's website, read news articles, and investigate reported cases on the LexisNexis database by using the search segment "counsel."

Dress as though you are interviewing for a job and plan to arrive a few minutes early. Bring extra copies of your résumé, transcript, and cover letter in case you are asked to furnish these during your meeting. Call or e-mail the day before to confirm your appointment.

The Interview

Informational interviews are not inquisitions, but rather a chance to converse and gain insight into another person's career path. Begin by shaking hands, introducing yourself, and expressing your thanks for the person's time.

The best questions explore a person's motivation for forging a particular career path. Some sample questions include:

- What motivated you to become a labor and employment law attorney?
- I'm interested to hear about your career path. Where did you work before this job?
- How did you obtain your first job? Can you describe your career track to me, including summer jobs and internships? Are there other ways to break into this field?
- What do you enjoy about this area of the law? Can you give me an example of an interesting case you've handled recently?
- What is a typical workday like for you?

- What do you enjoy the most about your work? Least?
- What types of skills are most valued by employers in this practice area? Should I focus on particular courses?
- What significant changes have you seen take place in this practice area through the years?
- What advice would you give someone just starting out in the profession?
- When hiring a new associate, what types of skills or experiences do you think are most important?
- Do you think a judicial clerkship would be a worthwhile experience?
- What professional associations would you recommend that I join?
- Do you know of others in this field whom I might contact?

When asking questions, be pleasant and attentive to the speaker. Take notes for future reference. Remember, you're having a conversation, so smile, nod, and make eye contact. The majority of your time ought to be spent listening, not speaking. "Don't worry if you don't get to talk too much," advises Mark Dighton, Director of School Relations for the Practising Law Institute in New York. "In fact, many lawyers will remember your conversation positively, even if you didn't say much, as long as you support what they say."

Follow-up

Send a thank-you note immediately following your interview. Try to personalize your note by making reference to the discussion during your meeting. For example:

> *Dear Ms. Katz,*
>
> *Thank you so much for taking the time to meet with me on Thursday to discuss your career path. I learned a great deal about labor and employment law practice in Northern New Jersey and will incorporate your suggestions in future job searches. In particular, I intend to join the*

New Jersey Bar Association's Section on Labor & Employment Law and will contact Fred Worth at Worth, Hooper & Smith about his work as a labor mediator. Hopefully, our paths will cross at a future bar association event. In the meantime, thank you for your time and advice. I appreciate it very much.

Sincerely,

Jane Networker

IN THEIR OWN WORDS...

Trust These Time-Tested Job Search Strategies

by Deborah Schneider
Co-author, *Should You Really Be A Lawyer? The Guide to Smart Career Choices Before, During and After Law School* (DecisionBooks, 2004) (www.shouldyoureally.com)

When I decided that I wanted to do career development work in a law school, I ran around and met with every law school career services director in the San Francisco Bay area. I got to know them and they got to know me. And everyone I met with said the same thing: "Too bad we didn't meet you six months ago, we were all hiring then. But don't worry, something will open."

Did those informational interviews take time? Yes. Did they turn into a job immediately? No. But did they pay off eventually? Absolutely.

A few months later, a career counselor at the University of San Francisco School of Law was going on maternity leave and the career services director called me to see if I wanted to fill in. Yes, I did.

While I was career counseling at USF Law, a permanent position opened up at UC Hastings College of the Law. Again, because she had already met me in an informational interview, the career services director called me to see if I wanted to apply for the position. Yes, I did!

I got that job and was again reminded about the power of informational interviews, networking, and, most of all, trusting that these time-tested job search strategies really work.

Cultivation

Keep a thorough record of your meeting, including contact information for your interviewee and for any other contacts who were suggested so that you can follow up again in the future. Chapter 5 will address tips and ideas for cultivating life-long networking contacts and growing your web of contacts over time.

IN THEIR OWN WORDS…

A First-hand Experience with Informational Interviewing

by Jake Samad
University of Pittsburgh '07

This past summer I had an externship with a judge in federal district court in Cincinnati. While I have enjoyed attending school in Pittsburgh, I know that I want to return to Cincinnati after law school. Because I knew that only a few Cincinnati firms conducted on-campus interviews at Pitt, I decided to make the most of my time in Cincinnati over the summer by scheduling informational interviews with interesting firms I knew would not be coming to Pittsburgh. I pooled my resources and found contacts at several different firms: the father of a former baseball teammate, a high school friend of my dad's, a friend of the office administrator at a firm where I used to work, and an alumnus of my high school. I basically cold-called each of these people — except for my dad's friend. Each call was met with an assistant or a voicemail box. I politely left messages saying who I was, how I came across the person's name, and that I was starting my job search and asking for a time to meet the person to discuss potential job search strategies. All four of the people I contacted responded and I met with all four of them.

Generally, the meetings took place at the person's office or over lunch. I came as prepared as I would have come for a job interview and was ready with questions concerning relocating, the local market, growing practice areas, grade requirements, etc. I found that after a few minutes of meeting me, the attorneys I spoke with were more than willing to share any thoughts or advice they had. The meetings generally lasted about 30 to 45 minutes. I came prepared with résumés, but instead of just handing over a résumé, I asked if the person wouldn't mind looking it over and offering any suggestions. I figured that this would be a little less forward and might end up opening a door or two. Immediately after the meetings, I went home and printed out thank you letters just as I would for any other interview thanking the attorneys for their time and their insights.

[Continued]

IN THEIR OWN WORDS... CONTINUED

Of the four attorneys I met, one painted a relatively bleak picture and didn't really offer much in the way of constructive advice. The other three, however, were extremely helpful. Two contacted me later and asked me to send them all of my materials and seemed interested in helping to get my name out to their associates. I ended up having interviews with both of these firms. Happily, I received an offer from one of the firms. Had it not been for the informational interview, I would not have had a chance at a job at this firm.

I am not sure exactly how this process might turn out for other people, but, personally, I found it extremely helpful. I learned a lot about the local market and about areas I might want to start looking into, and got to meet four extremely interesting people who may ultimately help me to find a job. I definitely had to make an investment and put myself out there a little bit, but the upside more than outweighs any potential negatives. I would recommend informational interviewing to anyone looking for work in the legal profession.

Chapter 5

Networking for Business Development and Career Growth

Landing your first job represents a tremendous milestone in your professional life. At long last, after years of study and networking to find the job of your dreams, you can focus on building practice skills as you embark on your first full-time job in the law.

While developing practice skills is important to your career success, you should also flex your networking muscles on a regular basis. Savvy networkers know that the process of creating and maintaining a circle of professional friends and acquaintances can influence your ability to find clients, create circles of influence, and help you secure your next position.

Fact: Your first job after law school will almost certainly not be your last. A study by the NALP Foundation (*Keeping the Keepers II: Mobility and Management of Associates*) reported that within the first two years of practice, nearly a quarter of the associates at law firms of all sizes have moved on. After five years, more than half of those hired directly out of law school have left their original firms.

Fact: Workers today can expect to hold approximately ten jobs during the course of their lives, according to studies by the Department of Labor's Bureau of Employment Statistics.[1]

---

1 *A Bureau of Labor Statistics news release published in August 2004 examined the number of jobs that people born in the years 1957 to 1964 held from age 18 to age 38. The title of the report is "Number of Jobs Held, Labor Market Activity, and Earnings Growth among Younger Baby Boomers: Results from More Than Two Decades of a Longitudinal Survey." The report is available on the BLS website at: http://www.bls.gov/news.release/pdf/nlsoy.pdf.*

These younger baby boomers held an average of 10.2 jobs from ages 18 to 38. (In this report, a job is defined as an uninterrupted period of work with a particular employer.) On average, men held 10.4 jobs and women held 9.9 jobs. Both men and women held more jobs on average in their late teens and early twenties than they held in their mid thirties.

From ages 18 to 38, some of these younger baby boomers held more jobs than average and others held fewer jobs. Twenty percent held 15 jobs or more, while 16 percent held zero to four jobs. For additional statistics on the number of jobs held, see the tables at: http://www.bls.gov/nls/y79r20jobsbyedu.pdf.

While networking is an important part of your job search, creating and fostering connections assumes even greater significance after graduation for several reasons. First, because you will probably change jobs more than once in your career, it makes sense to maintain and expand your circle of contacts who can alert you to job vacancies and other opportunities as they arise. Once law school ends, there will be no on-campus interview programs or weekly student newsletters announcing job openings. While professional legal recruiters can help identify opportunities, there is no substitute for personal networking contacts to vouch for your credentials and to learn about potential job openings.

> "All our dreams can come true if we have the courage to pursue them."
>
> — WALT DISNEY

Second, from a client-building perspective, the lawyers who are able to tap a wide array of contacts to attract business will only strengthen their position for both promotion and mobility. Lawyers who build client relationships and develop a book of business will realize greater compensation and mobility within the profession. "The more people you know, the greater your circle of influence, the greater chance that you will receive business referrals and build your practice," remarks Beth D. Tractenberg, a partner practicing trusts and estates law with Davies Ward Phillips & Vineberg in Manhattan.

Finally, maintaining a strong network of colleagues and contacts will help you during times of upheaval. During the course of your career, you will face a variety of challenges. The strength of your network will help support and sustain you during these times, so pay special attention to your friends and business colleagues following graduation.

Strategies to Build Your Network

The following suggestions will help guide you as you continue to cultivate and grow your network following graduation. Find the balance that's right for you and remember that networking is an incremental process that develops over a lifetime.

Set aside time each week to tend your network. Try to assign some time every week to cultivating and extending your circle of influence. By setting aside an hour or two, you guarantee that your efforts won't take place in fits and starts. For instance, decide that every week – each Friday perhaps – you will schedule a lunch with a former classmate, work colleague, or friend. If lunch doesn't work, try an early morning breakfast on a weekly basis.

Informal meetings with friends, former classmates, or colleagues enable you to develop relationships, exchange ideas, and secure bonds before you need help. Avoid "9-1-1" networking. No one enjoys being pumped for information or called upon in a crisis. By scheduling regular time each week to tend your network, you will develop a balanced give and take, establish trust, and avoid the reputation of being a "taker" who only calls upon friends during a catastrophe.

When you travel for business, make the time to schedule coffee or drinks with a colleague or friend from childhood, college, or law school. By carving out meeting times while traveling for work, you can continue to maintain connections and the face-to-face time, however brief, can eclipse any e-mail or telephone exchanges.

If you cannot find time each week to network, consider this creative solution from Diane K. Danielson, CEO of DowntownWomens Club.com and co-author of *Table Talk: The Savvy Girl's Alternative to Networking* (2003): Engage in "guerrilla networking" by going out several nights in succession and then engaging in follow-up activities for the next three months. Some people prefer to immerse themselves in a series of focused networking meetings, lunches, dinners, and cocktail events rather than setting aside time every week.

Find a mentor. One of the best ways to develop networking and business development skills is to find a mentor who will help teach you the fundamentals and guide you as you become a more experienced lawyer. To find a mentor, consider the lawyers in your firm, agency, or in-house legal department, or look beyond to your local bar association in order to find role models to guide you.

Marci Alboher, a lawyer and writer in Manhattan, praises the value of mentor relationships for new lawyers and also emphasizes the relevance of junior relationships. "Throughout your career you will shop for mentors," observes Alboher. "It's also important to spend time developing relationships with more junior lawyers in order to both lead and learn from the next generation."

IN THEIR OWN WORDS...

Creating a Mentoring Network

by Valerie A. Fontaine
Attorney, legal search professional, and author of *The Right Moves: Job Search and Career Development Strategies for Lawyers* (NALP, 2006)

To boost your career, it behooves you to have a mentoring network. Although having one powerful mentor can provide a number of advantages, having a network of mentors is much more beneficial. Mentors can advise and coach you, offer support, show you the ropes, introduce you to important contacts, and advocate for your advancement. Having a number of mentors, with a variety of backgrounds and strengths, increases your chances of being able to call upon the right person in the right place at the right time to help you move ahead.

The ideal is to create a network of mentors where you also mentor others in the group; you are both a mentor and a protégé at the same time. This network should be a dynamic web of contacts with varied expertise and experience, all of whom are willing and able to share their knowledge, cultural perspectives, and abilities. The contacts should be of various levels of seniority; even the most senior lawyer may be able to benefit from the fresh viewpoint of a more junior person. Determine what information and assistance you need from others and what you have to share. Even a very junior attorney can add value to a mentor-mentee relationship. Perhaps you can offer to assist with research for an article or presentation your mentor is preparing.

As your needs change over the course of your career, your network of mentors should grow accordingly. While you may outgrow your specific need for a particular mentor, you never outgrow the need for mentors. As you move up in your career, you face bigger challenges, and a sounding board and wise counsel will always be valuable.

Attend legal education programs. There's a great temptation, especially among new attorneys with a steep learning curve, to retreat to the office or law library and focus solely upon one's practice skills. While it is important to achieve excellence in practice fundamentals and develop specialized skills, to retreat from public view would be short-sighted.

If your state mandates compulsory continuing legal education, then attendance at legal education programs is an easy way to mix and mingle among colleagues while fulfilling your licensure requirements. If your state does not have mandatory CLE, consider attending seminars to improve your base of knowledge while socializing informally.

Become active in a bar association. For both law students and new lawyers, state, local, and specialty bar associations offer excellent opportunities to enlarge one's circle of contacts. Join your local Young Lawyers Division and attend some meetings to gauge your interest. In addition to educational programming, many Young Lawyers groups across the country participate in *pro bono* activities, including raising funds for local charities. In addition, many bar associations offer charitable giving opportunities that will enable you to take a leadership role in raising funds for a cause that impassions you. For instance, the Allegheny County Bar Association's Lawyers Against Hunger annual campaign welcomes new lawyers who volunteer to help raise awareness and funds for the local food bank.

Memberships in bar associations also enable you to stay current in your practice area, gain additional skills, and remain visible within your peer group. Joining a practice area section, committee, or division will enable you to meet lawyers from other law firms, government agencies, and in-house legal departments on both a social and professional level. Further, if you desire to learn more about a particular practice area with the hope of developing a specific area of practice (for example, you hope to practice entertainment law someday but currently you are in a general litigation firm), then joining a specific bar association section will help you make connections that may be helpful later in your career.

Whether you take continuing legal education programs, participate in advocacy initiatives, or simply socialize, bar association memberships will enlarge your circle and enable you to do good and to become known in your local legal community.

Private clubs. Private clubs – from dining and athletic clubs to country clubs – offer social and business development opportunities for new attorneys. Kim Lopez, a membership specialist with Dallas-based Club Corp, the largest club management company in the world, notes that "club membership is among the best ways to get connected in business and gain referral sources." Many private clubs offer networking events especially for club members, including lecture series, wine tasting events, athletic classes, and more. In some cities, law firms may encourage associates to become members of private clubs through special incentives (waived initiation fees or reduced monthly membership dues). Consider joining a club and participating in club governance. Whether you use the facilities for the dining privileges or the athletic programs, club memberships are yet another way to both socialize and mingle with like-situated individuals.

> "Go confidently [in] the direction o[f] your dreams. L[ive] the life you ha[ve] imagined."
>
> — HENRY DAVID THOREAU

Volunteer outside the legal community. A law firm partner once told me that bar associations are good places to become well-known among other lawyers, but to find new clients one ought to extend into the larger community. "When you're at a bar association event, you're in a room full of lawyers … not great for developing business of your own," said the partner. "But go to a Rotary luncheon or Kiwannis meeting and you might be the only lawyer in the room. … Suddenly you become a celebrity of sorts and an automatic authority on all things legal."

Network your way to career success and personal satisfaction by volunteering in your community. Whether coaching Little League, volunteering with the Girl Scouts, or taking a leadership role in your congregation, you will meet a wide range of people, from stay-at-home parents to corporate executives. Under the theory "you never know who people know," your participation in community activities – beyond the satisfaction of volunteering and playing an active role helping others – will enable you to socialize beyond the confines of the profession.

"Networking and collegiality in business or personal relationships outside of legal representation are essential to establishing a reputation and growing a practice," notes attorney Deborah A. Scalise with Jones Garneau, LLP in Scarsdale, NY. "Successful lawyers are oriented toward their community – not only the legal community, but also the local community. Along with participation in bar associations and other business groups (such as Rotary, Kiwannis or the Lions Club), lawyers volunteer to work with children, the elderly, charities, or political campaigns. Such activities are not only rewarding in and of themselves but also enhance the reputation of the individual lawyer or law firm – and, perhaps more importantly, of the profession as a whole. Lawyers and law firms who regularly set aside time to engage in community activities will develop trusting relationships, thereby allowing those who know and like them to request assistance with legal issues. In turn, such activities will reward the lawyer and/or law firm with a successful practice."

Diane K. Danielson advises, "When attending events beyond the legal community, be ready to describe your work with an easy-to-understand 'signature line.' For instance, instead of saying that you practice mergers and acquisitions law, tell people that you help buy and sell companies in China. Most lawyers spend time around other lawyers and assume a level of understanding about practice areas. Be able to describe what you do to a layperson and connect."

Volunteer opportunities abound, and some of the following options may appeal to you:

- Political party affiliations
- Alumni organizations
- Religious congregations (church, synagogue, mosque, or other spiritual association) and religious-oriented advocacy groups
- Business-related groups such as Kiwannis, Rotary, or Lions Club
- Parent-teacher associations, school boards, or other civic service within your community

- Children's sporting programs in baseball, hockey, basketball, soccer, or football
- Social/fundraising organizations such as Masonic Lodge, Junior League, Hadassah, or the American Association of University Women
- Groups that might appeal to your sense of values and interests, such as the Sierra Club, Boys and Girls Clubs of America, or the American Civil Liberties Union

Participate in alumni events. When you receive invitations to alumni get-togethers for either your law school or college, make an effort to attend these events. Whether it's a lecture featuring a noted scholar, a sporting event, or a happy hour, alumni programs put you in contact with individuals who share at least one credential in common: their school affiliation. It's a low-risk proposition to make the time to attend. You may learn something new, reconnect with old friends, or meet someone new who might influence you in a positive way. Other ways to participate include:

- Serving on the planning committee for future alumni events and taking a leadership role in creating programming for your classmates.
- Becoming a mentor to law students. Many career services and alumni affairs offices offer mentor programs to students. Your participation will help link the next generation of young lawyers to the profession and beyond. By making yourself available, you can help teach a new professional and reconnect to your law school.
- Participating on a law school career services panel to share information about your career path, tips, and ideas for successful practice.

Be a reliable referral source. Be ready to provide lawyer referrals. In my experience, lawyers are most frequently asked for advice about either family or real estate law. In an informal social context, few people have ever asked me to recommend a mergers and acquisitions attorney or questioned my knowledge of the state tax code, but everyone wants to know the names of the most reputable divorce lawyers or needs quick answers about real estate agreements. Do yourself a favor:

If you're not sure, ask around and keep a list of three or four names to offer when asked for referrals in these areas. By becoming an authority and being "in the know," you increase your chances that when another legal question arises, the person you helped will be favorably disposed to tapping your expertise again, and this might result in billable client work for you.

Accountants, insurance agents, and bankers. Work on fostering trusting relationships with accountants, insurance agents and bankers. These professionals are prime referral sources for private practitioners because they can refer clients. Attorney Beth D. Tractenberg recalls, "My business development as a trusts and estates attorney blossomed with referrals to and from accountants, bankers, and insurance professionals. Get to know professionals whom you trust in these industries and leverage those relationships to build your business."

IN THEIR OWN WORDS...

Lessons Learned by Successful Women Lawyers

by Phyllis Horn Epstein
Partner, Epstein, Shapiro & Epstein, P.C., Philadelphia, PA

The following is an excerpt from Women-at-Law: Lessons Learned Along the Pathways to Success (ABA, 2006). *Reprinted with permission.*

Men have always networked by attending professional sporting events, golfing, or joining wine tasting clubs. During her hiatus from the full-time practice of law, [U.S. District Judge Norma Shapiro] became active with her local school board, from which she began developing a wider circle of contacts that ultimately benefited her when she sought endorsement for her elevation to the bench. To be known by others is to have the makings of a future client base and sources of business referrals.

Women should participate in professional organizations like the American Bar Association, as well as local bar associations. I have been a member of the ABA Taxation Section for nearly 20 years and by doing so have expanded my professional network of tax lawyers to men and women across the country. I have been able to refer legal matters to others with specific tax expertise and have had matters referred back to me. The continuing legal education within the organization is at an expert level. There is an energy — a synergy — that emerges from gathering with peers in legal symposiums. Our bar associations have much to offer and a myriad of ways to participate.

> Never, never, never, never give up.
>
> — WINSTON CHURCHILL

A word about golf. Once solely the domain of wealthy men, golf is becoming a popular sport for anyone who wants to cultivate business, entertain colleagues, and socialize informally. While golf is not the only way to cement business contacts and engage your colleagues, this sport has a certain appeal, particularly among lawyers. Regardless of your age, it's never too late to learn the fundamentals and ascertain if this sport is a good fit for you. The United States Golf Association (www.usga.org) offers a comprehensive website with resources about teachers, rules, and a history of the game.

According to the National Golf Foundation, there are 12.8 million adult golfers in the U.S. who play at least eight times per year. Of this group of core golfers, 10.2 million are male and 2.5 million are female. As of December 31, 2004, there were 16,057 golf facilities, 11,690 of which were open to the public. The states with the most golf facilities are Florida, California, Texas, Michigan, and New York.

In 2003, Catalyst, a nonprofit organization, conducted a survey of women in Fortune 1,000 companies about the impediments they felt were preventing them from succeeding in the workplace. More than 40 percent cited "exclusion from informal networks" as a barrier to their success. One of the most-cited informal networks was golf.

According to attorney Suzanne Woo, author of *On Course for Business: Women & Golf* (John Wiley & Sons), golf enables you to strengthen ties with clients and advance your business relationships. Woo, who began to take golf lessons during her second year of law school, advises lawyers to "take up the game for stress reduction … and also because the fact that you can 'talk the game' builds rapport with business colleagues."

To learn more about golf instruction and networking opportunities for women, consider the following organizations:

- Golfingwomen (www.golfingwomen.com) offers business-golf workshops, personal coaching, and an eight-hour crash course called Tee Off Tomorrow.

- Executive Women's Golf Association (www.ewga.com) provides clinics for all skill levels, including new golfers, as well as rules and etiquette seminars throughout the U.S. and Canada.
- Bizgolf Dynamics (www.bizgolf.biz) offers seminars and consultations for new and experienced golfers.

Writing, publishing, and speaking. Build your reputation through writing and speaking engagements. As a new lawyer, you may have difficulty finding the time to write articles or speak at professional events. However, even young lawyers can write by volunteering for bar association assignments – drafting copy for letters, proposals, even taking minutes at meetings. Similarly, your speaking engagements may start small (perhaps at a high school program discussing the fundamentals of constitutional law), but your confidence and reputation will grow with each passing year as you develop expertise and experience. Many public libraries offer free programs on a wide array of topics, from divorces and wills and trusts to first amendment issues. Inquire at your local library about the possibility of your sharing information about yourself and your firm.

Make regular deposits in the "Favor Bank." One good turn deserves another, and this sentiment is particularly apropos in the networking world. While it's important to be kind and thoughtful regardless of the consequences, networking mavens know that you need to reciprocate as well as ask for referrals. Timothy E. Parks, Director of Business Development for the Business & Finance Group at Morgan, Lewis & Bockius LLP, likens this give and take to transactions in a metaphorical Favor Bank. Make sure that you make deposits as well as withdrawals from time to time. By keeping tabs on your personal balance in the Favor Bank, you can help yourself and others to information and connections when an opportunity arises.

Schedule Your Networking Efforts

With the pressures of adjusting to your new career, you may be tempted to forgo regular networking efforts. After all, you might say, who has time for developing and fostering connections? Simply put, make the time. By scheduling regular time during your work week to network with colleagues and new contacts, you will develop a life-long habit that will benefit you throughout your career. Many expert networkers recommend that you spend some time each day building and cultivating your network. As with daily exercise, those who can discipline themselves to carve out time each day will reap the benefits.

Many experienced networkers refer to the process of reaching out to contacts as making "touches" or "taps." These are informal, intermittent ways to keep yourself in others' minds in a positive way. In the words of the old telephone jingle, "reach out and touch someone."

The following are suggestions for generating regular "touches" with your ever-expanding circle of contacts:

- Keep accurate records of your networking contacts. If you maintain lists on your personal computer, PalmPilot®, Filofax®, or notebook, be sure to update your data on a regular basis. This way, when you need to generate a mailing list for a professional announcement or are compiling an invitation list to your law firm's tenth anniversary party, your information on contacts is accessible and up to date.
- Develop your own annual plan for making regular contacts with your networking base throughout the year. Many lawyers and law firms send holiday cards as part of a regular, seasonal "touch" by mail. Others send Thanksgiving greetings to clients ahead of the holiday rush. Brian Degan, a 2004 Suffolk Law graduate who works for the Boston Red Sox baseball organization, likes to write to his networking contacts on opening day. "Everyone gets holiday cards and not everyone reads them or feels obligated to respond but by finding a day that is not surrounded by chaos and clutter, your note will receive more attention and seem more personal," says Degan. Decide what works best for you and commit to a plan of action.

> "If you are serious about improving your relationships with other people, get in the habit of writing notes — by hand — especially notes that say 'thank you,' 'I'm sorry,' 'congratulations,' and 'I can really sympathize with your sorrow.' Writing notes gets you in the habit of true thoughtfulness and makes you look quite special, especially as the popularity of handwriting a note wanes. Indeed, it is the habit that is easy to lose in our digital, fast-paced age but just as easy to reacquire. So remember this maxim. Failure to write a thank you note can fail to improve relationships and may risk hurting one, especially with an older person. The lesson here: When in doubt, handwrite it out."
> — Larry and Susan Terkel, authors of *Small Change*

- Every day, make at least one friendly phone call to a colleague or friend to check in. How often do you groan to yourself when you get a phone call from a distant acquaintance asking for something (your time, your money, your influence)? Don't be an opportunistic individual who only calls when there's something you need. A casual call to inquire after a friend or classmate, perhaps with an invitation to lunch, will be a welcome departure from the typical phone call with strings attached. Develop a reputation for graciousness by making friendly inquiries with no strings attached once a day.
- Depending on your firm and practice area, consider creating a regular e-newsletter to send to clients, potential clients, and colleagues describing recent developments in the law and your practice area.
- Develop the habit of recognizing personal and professional accomplishments and milestones of your colleagues and friends. Buy an array of greeting cards to have on hand for birthdays, anniversaries, and birth announcements, and to convey sympathy. Mark recurring dates on your calendar, computer, or PDA. You build goodwill when you take a moment each day to review upcoming events and send cards to friends and colleagues.
- Become a news referral source. If you know a classmate or colleague is interested in a particular topic and you read about it in the newspaper, either clip the article and send it with a personal note or simply e-mail it with personal greetings. The best networkers are people who are perceived to be "in the know." Therefore, build your reputation as a news referral source by thinking of others and being on the

lookout for stories that will interest your colleagues. For example, if you know your law school classmate enjoys fine dining and is moving to Chicago, send her the link to the Zagat's site in Chicago with a personal note. Or, better yet, consider buying her the latest guide to Chicago restaurants with a handwritten note of congratulations.

- Take advantage of any access you have to tickets to theater, sporting events, and concerts. If you are a new lawyer and your firm encourages you to do so, consider entertaining current or potential clients. A social evening spent at a baseball game can help cement a business friendship or build the foundation for future referrals.

Follow-up

A single networking "touch" is only the beginning. Conducting consistent follow-up will keep you focused and enhance your circle of networking opportunities. Prompt yourself with notes on your weekly calendar to make follow-up inquiries. For instance, following a lunch meeting with a contact, be sure to send a brief e-mail that day saying "great to see you" and then mark your calendar to issue another invitation in two months' time.

A *Minneapolis Star Tribune* jobs section article by Matt Krumrie emphasizes that the number one way to make the most of your networking time is to engage in follow-up. Here are some ideas Krumrie offers for following up with contacts:

- Always send a thank you note.
- Ask colleagues to subscribe to your e-newsletter.
- Cut out a relevant article and mail it to them.
- E-mail them with some relevant information.
- Call them.
- Send a referral.

In addition to follow-up actions, a regular part of your networking plan should include a periodic review of your list of contacts to determine which should remain and which have become stale with time. Keeping your networking list fresh and current will focus your energies. If you cannot recall a person's face or your reason for having their name in the first place, or if you have attempted three times to make contact and have failed to do so, then consider removing the name from your list of networking contacts. The trail has grown cold and you ought to focus on developing other prospects.

Your object is not to have the largest contact list in the world but instead to have a carefully honed list of individuals whom you know, who know you, and who are cultivated through regular meetings, e-mails, letters, and social and professional events. Think of your growing network in terms of concentric circles of influence. Your innermost circle ought to encompass your family, closest friends and colleagues with whom you share a special bond, and your "go to" support system of mentors and confidantes. Your intermediate circle of contacts will be larger and should include your work friends, college and law school classmates with whom you were friendly, neighbors, friends from the gym, and other familiar but not particularly close contacts. Finally, your outermost circle will be general acquaintances as well as those you hope to connect with but have not yet reached.

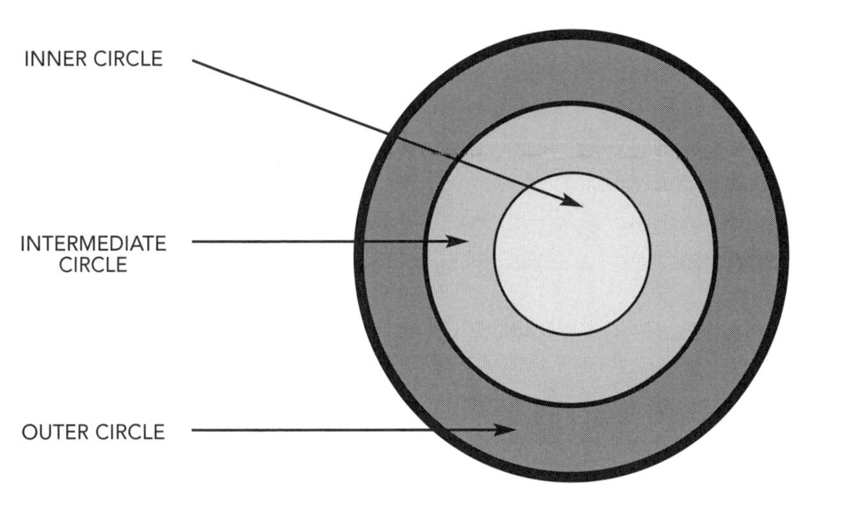

As you develop and nurture your network of contacts, the individuals in the various circles of influence will shift over time. By keeping close tabs on where certain individuals fall in the continuum, you will better manage your ever-growing network of personal and professional contacts.

IN THEIR OWN WORDS...

Networking Tips for Women

by Deborah Epstein Henry, Esq.
Founder and President, Flex-Time Lawyers LLC
(www.flextimelawyers.com)

Business development and marketing are all about networking. Networking is all about building relationships and connections. If you ask anyone whether women or men are better at developing relationships, the majority will say that women are more relational and connected than men. If this is so, then why are women lawyers not reaching the same levels of success in business development and marketing as their male colleagues?

What follows are suggested ideas about how to get started, including general networking tips:

- Take an inventory of existing contacts you have, both personal and professional. In developing a list of these people, note who you know, who your contacts know, and who you would like to meet through your contacts.
- Ask your mentors and colleagues as well as people in your library or marketing department about where existing business comes from in your firm and practice area. This is critical because before being effective in developing business, lawyers need to know their target audience.
- Single out rainmakers in your firm and learn from them or other sources how they have developed their client base.
- Speak with mentors and friends outside the firm about how they have developed business or how their colleagues have had success in doing so.
- Research what meetings and conferences are attended by those in your practice area and target audience.
- Read CLE brochures, announcements in legal publications, and recognitions and awards to learn who is at the forefront of the issues concerning you and your practice.
- Research what publications are "must reads" for those in your practice area (both by partners and in-house counsel).
- Determine if there are opportunities to write articles for these publications as part of non-billable work you are already expected to do for your firm.

[Continued]

IN THEIR OWN WORDS... (CONTINUED)

- Initiate mentoring relationships with different types of people for whom you have done work or for whom you would like to work or whom you otherwise admire.
- Develop a relationship with the assigning partner and/or administrator in charge of assigning cases. These people are instrumental in your professional development because they help determine both the type of work you do and the colleagues with whom you work.
- Develop a relationship with the marketing person at your place of employment because that person may be instrumental in helping you market yourself both internally and externally.

IN THEIR OWN WORDS...

Staying Networked

by Rebecca Zucker
Principal of Next Step Partners, an executive coaching and leadership development firm

In this tough job market, no one has to tell you how important it is to network. If you don't know that, you are either independently wealthy and don't ever need to work, or you've been hiding under a rock for the bulk of your career.

What a lot of people don't recognize, until they are faced with a job search, is that it pays to stay networked — particularly in good times, when you don't feel the need as much to keep in touch. Staying networked on a regular basis will put you steps ahead of everyone who has not remained connected when it comes time for a job search or getting the information or resources you need.

While most people are happy to help you by either taking time to meet with you or spend a few minutes to chat on the phone, their time is limited — and no one likes a fair-weather friend, acquaintance, or colleague. It is uncomfortable for both parties to become reconnected only when one person needs something from the other. This may work once, but it rarely works twice.

Aside from the obvious efforts to join industry associations or attend alumni events, there are some simple, yet highly effective, ways to stay connected and build stronger professional relationships.

Let others know what you're up to. This can be done easily by e-mail or in a holiday card, for example. By letting someone know things like "I recently relocated to Chicago to do strategic planning for XYZ Corporation ...," you are also letting them know that you'd like to keep in touch with them. Most will be flattered that you kept them up to date and won't be as surprised to hear from you if you do call them in the future for a favor.

[Continued]

IN THEIR OWN WORDS... (CONTINUED)

Go to lunch. It's easy to get consumed at work or in your daily activities and just inhale a sandwich at your desk. However, by making a point to go to lunch at least once or twice a week with a friend or colleague who works at your firm or elsewhere, you can not only stay in touch, but you can also find out what's happening with other people and other companies.

Call classmates and colleagues when you are traveling on business. Not only does this beat eating a cold deli sandwich in your hotel room, it is a great way to stay in touch and find out what's going on with friends and colleagues. Be sure to reciprocate the invitation when they are in your city on business or holiday.

Give others something they need. This is best done unsolicited, but is just as important when someone asks you for help. Whether it is putting people in contact with a potential employer, client, partner, etc., or giving them information that could be useful for them, they will remember your generosity and return the favor. For example, by sending people information on an upcoming conference in their field that they may not already be aware of, with a note attached ("I thought you might be interested in this ..."), you remind them of your presence and demonstrate your willingness to help them. Once again, most people will be flattered that you thought of them.

Take leadership positions. Whether is it at your church or synagogue, leading a task force at your company, or planning an event for your alumni association, assuming a leadership position gives you the ability to (1) meet diverse groups of professionals, (2) be seen and known by others, and (3) call members of these groups and ask them for information, help, etc.

Connect others. By putting other people in touch and helping them to broaden their networks, you are helping them expand the realm of people that they can, in turn, put you in touch with. They will also remember the favor and return it one day.

Help others succeed. If the saying goes, "It pays to know people in high places," then help others attain these high places, so you can know these people.

If you stay connected on a regular basis, people will start to come to you as a source of information. People will say, "Call Jane — she knows everyone." Or, "Call Bob, he always knows what people are up to." When you've achieved and maintained this level of connection with others, your call to them will seem far less of an imposition than it might have if you hadn't made these ongoing efforts to stay connected.

Chapter 6

Networking and the Nontraditional Legal Career

Nontraditional legal careers continue to grow in popularity as law graduates realize that a law degree opens doors to many other career paths apart from traditional practice. Nontraditional careers encompass a wide range of options from the law-related fields of legal placement, teaching, politics, and lobbying to careers in consulting, business, retail management, writing, banking, social work, and beyond. By taking "the road less traveled," you open yourself up to a world of possibilities.

The challenge for most law graduates contemplating a nontraditional career path is choosing from the variety of options and finding the right fit for your particular skills and interests. Nontraditional careers are not a "one size fits all" proposition, and a tremendous amount of time, energy, and exploration ought to be spent considering different options. The lawyer pursuing a nontraditional path is often forging a new path, and the traditional job-searching models that are taught in law school (on-campus interviewing and responding to job postings, chief among them) will not work.

If you are contemplating a nontraditional career path, networking can help you achieve your goal. "When contemplating a nontraditional career, you need to forge your own career path and create connections through a strong network," observes Marci Alboher. Alboher left law practice to become a journalist in late 1999 after nearly a decade of practicing advertising and consumer law. As a regular contributor to *The New York Times*, she writes primarily about workplace trends and business travel. In 2002, she wrote her first book, *I Think I Need a Lawyer, Now What?* (Silver Lining Books), a layperson's guide to the law. She is currently at work on a second book about career choices.

"When looking to get my book published, I networked with everyone I'd ever met – friends, family, and even my dentist!" relates Brenda Janowitz, lawyer-turned-novelist. "Friends put me in touch with their friends in publishing, who gave me invaluable advice – the sorts of things you wouldn't know about the business unless you spoke to a true insider – and that advice helped me to conduct a smart search for an agent. I also learned the etiquette involved when seeking an agent (which was much different from what I knew from searching for a job as an attorney) and how to properly research agents. When agents began contacting me with interest in my book, I then had a group of industry professionals at the ready with thoughtful opinions and advice."

> "Two roads diverged in a wood, and I — I took the one less traveled by. And that has made all the difference."
>
> — ROBERT FROST "The Road Not Tak

Networking can ease the transition to nontraditional practice. Heather Lewis-Lechner, a graduate of Seattle University School of Law, works as the Policy Counsel for the Senate Democratic Caucus in Olympia, Washington. According to Lewis-Lechner, the key to identifying nontraditional opportunities is networking. She recommends getting to know people in the area who do the type of work you think you would like to pursue. "Network, network, network. As cheesy as that sounds, it's true. I've found that, in the nontraditional areas that I was looking at – political and nonprofit work – the positions are often hard to find if you don't know someone who already works there and if they don't already know you. Volunteer work in the area you are considering is always a good way to get your foot in the door, start to know and establish relationships with people in the arena you are looking at, and find out about all the options that may be available. You definitely have to take the initiative in order to get noticed and stand out."

Brian Degan, a 2004 graduate of Suffolk Law School, works for the Boston Red Sox, a dream job for anyone contemplating a career in sports management. Degan approached his nontraditional job search by networking with a wide range of individuals. He began by composing an extensive list of attorneys and conducting informational interviews.

"When meeting with contacts I told them bluntly that I needed their help, wanted their help, and would do all the leg work if they would just be kind enough to introduce me or give me permission to use their name when calling or writing to someone. ... I wanted to give each contact the impression that they were the only professional that I was meeting with." Through networking and informational interviews, Degan succeeded in finding a management position with the Boston Red Sox.

When contemplating a nontraditional career path, consider the following tips and begin to embrace a network of like-minded individuals who can help guide you.

Research nontraditional careers. Before leaping into nontraditional work, consider your motivations for doing so and become comfortable with your decision. Rather than saying "I hate practicing law," you will likely find a more hospitable reception from potential nonlegal employers if you're able to say "I have the following transferable skills and have decided, after lots of exploration, that this is the right path for me...."

Deborah L. Arron's *What Can You Do With A Law Degree?* (DecisionBooks) is, in my opinion, one of the best books published on the topic of nontraditional legal careers. Arron describes the decision-making process and engages the reader in the process of values clarification, goal-setting, and resources. Arron also wrote *Running from the Law: Why Good Lawyers Are Getting Out of the Legal Profession* (DecisionBooks), a collection of interviews with respected ex-practicing attorneys who gave up promising legal careers. The appendices contain tips on career planning and finding support and recommended resources.

Other good resources about nontraditional career paths include:

- *Nonlegal Careers for Lawyers,* by Gary A. Munneke, William D. Henslee, and Ellen Wayne (American Bar Association, 2006).
- *Should Your Really Be a Lawyer? The Guide to Smart Career Choices Before, During, and After Law School,* by Deborah Schneider (DecisionBooks, 2005).

- *The Lawyer's Career Change Handbook: More than 300 Things You Can Do with a Law Degree,* by Hindi Greenberg (Avon, 2002).
- *Beyond L.A. Law: Break The Traditional "Lawyer" Mold,* Janet Smith, editor (Harcourt Brace Legal & Professional Publications, 1998).
- *Changing Jobs: A Handbook for Lawyers,* by Carol M. Kanarek, editor (American Bar Association Young Lawyers Division, 1988).
- *Full Disclosure – Do You Really Want to Be a Lawyer?* by Susan J. Bell (American Bar Association, 1992).
- *JD Preferred: Legal Career Alternatives* (Federal Reports Inc., 1995).

Finally, *Non-Traditional Legal Career Report* (www.nontradlegal.com) is published every two weeks and lists positions for J.D.'s in non-law firm settings. Over 90 law schools currently subscribe to the *Report*, and the online version is available as a subscription service. Archived editions will remain available as a resource to lawyers and law students considering nontraditional options. If your law school does not subscribe, individual subscriptions are available at a cost of $40 for three months. Write to Career Education Institutes, P.O. Box 11171, Winston-Salem, NC 27116 and include your e-mail address to receive individual access codes.

In addition to reading, find lawyers who have chosen nontraditional career paths and conduct informational interviews (see chapter 4 for details) to determine if the path in which you're interested is the right path for you.

Connect with your career services office. Visit your career services office and seek advice about nontraditional options. Many law school career counselors are former practicing lawyers and may be able to provide valuable advice and names of graduates who have forged similar paths. Most career services offices welcome back graduates, typically without fee.

In addition to your career services office, research whether your local bar association provides career counseling. Some bar associations offer free career counseling and skills testing, such as the Myers-Briggs Type

Indicator. Take advantage of these services to determine your strengths, weaknesses, and areas of interest as you explore nontraditional options.

Take classes and connect with a new peer group. If you are trying to make a career change and want to test drive your ideas, register for classes in your particular area of interest. For instance, if you are a litigation associate who dreams about opening a restaurant, consider taking classes at the local culinary institute. You will learn hands-on skills, meet individuals with similar interests, and study with a seasoned professional who might be a helpful source of information. When Marci Alboher began to transition from traditional practice to life as a writer, she took journalism and writing classes, went to writer meetings and author events, and formed friendships with writers. In short, Alboher created her own community of like-minded individuals who were focused on a similar goal. The result: an article in *The New York Times* followed by a stint as a contributing editor for American Lawyer Media, and a new book about – what else? – lawyers who transition into other careers.

Join organizations and associations. "Involvement with professional associations, especially for career-changers, may offer the single best source of opportunities to develop a lot of new networking contacts from one source," observes Hal Flantzer, President of Professional Career Resources in New York City. "It also gives you a great way to keep yourself current with the latest developments in your field. Professional associations are also well aware – and supportive – of the need for their members and potential members to network. In fact, they will set aside time at the beginning of chapter meetings for just that purpose. Active involvement, i.e., joining committees, writing articles for newsletters, etc., will enable you to get positive exposure – and enhance your positioning, as well as open up greater opportunities to meet new colleagues. More importantly, you will be able to develop the type of collegial relationships that will move your career along, well beyond the time that you land your next position or consulting engagement."

Describe your transferable skills. The research, writing, and analytical skills you acquired in law school have great relevance to nontraditional employers. Don't feel that you have to disregard three years of graduate school study in order to shift to a nonlegal career path. Evaluate your marketable skills and be sure to discuss these skills with potential employers.

When drafting résumés and cover letters for nontraditional jobs, consider diverging from the traditional law school résumé model and create a skills-based résumé instead. This way, instead of highlighting legal employment, you can focus on specific skills that you might bring to a nontraditional employer. Similarly, cover letters addressed to nontraditional employers should emphasize your skills and de-emphasize your legal training.

Staying connected to the legal profession. Remaining a part of the legal profession is a deeply personal decision and depends, in large measure, on the type of nontraditional work you seek to pursue, your resources, and values. Whether to ditch it all depends upon your individual circumstances. If you open a country inn, then perhaps keeping your license and going to professional events doesn't make sense anymore. However, if you are pursuing a career in legal recruitment, then keeping a professional presence may be merited because you will be dealing with lawyers as a part of your new enterprise.

Give yourself some time to test the waters before you surrender your license and cut all ties. The time, energy, and money required to move from "inactive" status to "active" status can be daunting so, at least in the short-term, consider keeping your professional license. I have kept my license to practice in Pennsylvania and will continue to do so. Why? I write about the legal profession, spend time interviewing lawyers and counseling law students, and speak to audiences of law students and lawyers. I feel that my professional credentials give me additional credence when I write or give presentations. I depend on lawyers and law students to speak with me frankly, and I want them to know that I'm in their club.

Persistence. Navigating the world of nontraditional career choices requires great persistence and energy. By taking the time to research, investigate, conduct informational interviews, and network, you will find a satisfying career path that is beyond the typical legal career.

IN THEIR OWN WORDS...

Networking and the Nontraditional Job Search

by Gina Sauer, J.D.

Career Coach & Marketing Director, The Esquire Group, Minneapolis, MN

Networking during the process of looking for an alternative or nontraditional legal position is arguably even more critical than it is when seeking a position within the traditional practice of law. If you're looking for a traditional position, you probably already have a good handle on what a bankruptcy attorney does or what a position as a litigator would entail, and you already know a lot about that career path — from law clerk to associate to partner. That's pretty much a given. And by the time you graduate from law school, you generally understand the application and hiring process in a law firm, and you can ask your career services office for information on typical pay scales. You also know what skills a traditional lawyer needs and can tailor your résumé accordingly. So the primary purpose of networking in the context of traditional, practicing jobs is simply to meet the right person on the right day, who may know of the right job.

When looking for an alternative position, however, networking is as much about educating yourself as it is about meeting people who may know of an opening. Most law students and lawyers with "alternative" aspirations probably don't know what the natural career progression is for a legal analyst or contract negotiator, and in many cases there may not even be a standard, defined career path. Most alternative job seekers likewise may not know where those types of positions can typically be found, what the application process is like, what they pay, and what skills sets are most valued by those employers. Gathering this type of information will make you much more savvy, while at the same time introducing you to people who may be able to connect you with a job.

Epilogue

Through networking, you have the power to widen your circle of acquaintances, gain valuable information about your career choices, and enrich your life. Regardless of your grades, your prior work experience, or your socio-economic background, you can create connections and enhance your career opportunities.

Follow these steps for networking success:

- Identify your personal network.
- Broaden your networking circle beyond your personal contacts.
- Learn to socialize with confidence.
- Find a personal networking style that works for you.
- Conduct informational interviews.
- Follow up and acknowledge.
- Be a referral source and ask for referrals in return.
- Create an annual networking plan.

Use the tools in this book to make a difference in your life. And remember, when someone says, "you ought to talk to so-and-so," don't cringe. Instead, take the name and contact information and follow up. You may be pleasantly surprised to find that the world is more interconnected than you ever imagined.

I wish you the very best. While luck is sometimes a factor in career success, there is no substitute for hard work, persistence, and the courage to ask others for information and assistance. Now put down the book, pick up the phone, call a friend or colleague, and connect.

Bibliography

Continue to build your career connections by reading:

Bowling Alone: The Collapse and Revival of American Community by Robert D. Putnam (Simon & Schuster, 2000).

Business Notes: Writing Personal Notes that Build Professional Relationships by Florence Isaacs (Clarkson Potter, 1998).

Dig Your Well Before You're Thirsty: The Only Networking Book You'll Ever Need by Harvey Mackay (Doubleday, 1997).

How to Create Your Own Luck: The You Never Know Approach to Networking, Taking Chances, and Opening Yourself to Opportunity by Susan RoAne (John Wiley & Sons, Inc., 2004).

How to Win Friends and Influence People by Dale Carnegie (1936). A true classic.

How to Work a Room: The Ultimate Guide to Savvy Socializing in Person and Online by Susan RoAne (Harper Collins, 2000).

Just a Note to Say … The Perfect Words for Every Occasion by Florence Isaacs (Clarkson Potter, 1995).

Networking by Douglas B. Richardson (John Wiley & Sons, Inc., 1994). Part of the *Wall Street Journal/National Business Employment Weekly Premier Guides.*

Networking for Job Search and Career Success by L. Michelle Tullier (JIST Works, 2004).

Never Eat Alone: And Other Secrets to Success, One Relationship at a Time by Keith Ferrazzi (Doubleday, 2005).

Nonstop Networking: How to Improve Your Life, Luck, and Career by Andrea R. Nierenberg (Capital Books, 2002).

Power Networking: 55 Secrets for Personal and Professional Success by Donna Fisher and Sandy Vilas (Mountain Harbor Publications, 1992).

Small Change by Lawrence Terkel and Susan Terkel (Tarcher/Penguin, 2004).

Supernetworking: Reach the Right People, Build Your Career Network, and Land Your Dream Job – Now! by Michael Salmon (The Career Press, 2004).

The Networking Survival Guide: Get the Success You Want by Tapping into the People You Know by Diane Darling (McGraw Hill, 2003).

The Right Moves: Job Search and Career Development Strategies for Lawyers by Valerie A. Fontaine (NALP, 2006).

What Do I Say Next? Talking Your Way to Business and Social Success by Susan RoAne (Warner Books, 1997).

Web-Based Networking Resources

www.careerbuilder.com is a collaboration among Gannett Co., Inc., Knight-Ridder, and Tribune Company. More than 90 Gannett newspapers are now CareerBuilder.com affiliates. With a presence in over 200 local markets, CareerBuilder.com has nationwide postings.

www.classmates.com is a service of Classmates Online, Inc. Founded in 1995, this website focuses on online social networking based on listings from over 200,000 schools.

www.craigslist.org, developed by Craig Newmark, is an online community that offers a variety of opportunities to meet and network via cyberspace at no charge.

www.LinkedIn.com is a free online networking resource that enables you to tap into a network of contacts based on city and profession. Your contact information is never made public. When people contact you through LinkedIn, you can decide whether or not to accept the contact and share your contact information with them.

www.monster.com offers thousands of job postings, as well as career information and advice for free.

www.ryze.com helps people make connections and grow their networks. Basic membership is free; paid subscriptions offer advanced features. Members get a free networking-oriented home page and can send messages to other members. They can also join special Networks related to their industry, interests, or location.

www.zerodegrees.com offers a search engine that helps you capitalize on existing connections and identifies new networking contacts. You must register and complete a profile. Currently, services are free.

www.thesquare.com is the online network of alumni and students from the world's most selective colleges and universities. Founded in 1997, TheSquare was acquired in 2001 and has expanded its services to create the **TheSquare Network**, consisting of TheSquare, SquareDating, and SquareJobs. Membership is free of charge, but only verified students and alumni of a select list of schools are eligible.

Acknowledgments

What would a book about networking be without giving thanks to a veritable cast of thousands who helped advise me and foster professional and personal connections?

Thank you to: Marci Alboher, Harold Behar, Michele Bendekovic, Erin Binns, David Blaner, Lisa Bluestein, Elaine M. Bourne, Ron Brown, Alexandria Bullara, Maureen Kelly Busis, Brian Chevlin, Mary Kate Coleman, Colleen Davis, Pamela Day, Brian Degan, Lisa Dickinson, Sylvia Diez and the Women's Leadership Forum at the Rivers Club in Pittsburgh, PA, Mark Dighton, Lori Dowling, Demetrious Eleftheriou, Suzanne Endrizzi, Phyllis Horn Epstein, Debra Fine, Scott Fingal, Valerie Fontaine, David Gerson, Gary Gittelman, Kevin Grierson, Jeanne M. Hammerstrom, Deborah Epstein Henry, Elene Herskowitz, Lynda Heyman, Brenda Janowitz, Alison Karpel, Caroline Kelly, Nancy Jackson Klucher, Robin Kushner, Matt Krumrie, Carole Langsam (my mother), Mimi Laver, Temma Lipsitz, Carolyn Weisberger Mendelson, Sheri Minkoff, Christine E. Miller, Debbie Moidel, Martha Neil, Lisa Oleinick, Judy Palkovitz, Timothy E. Parks, Ira Pilchen, Matthew L. Pascocello, Amy Pople, Kristen McManus Powers, Susan RoAne, Judy Rosemarin, Jake Samad, Gina Sauer, Deborah A. Scalise, Deborah Schneider, Jan Shaw, the late James Smith III, Janet Smith, Michelle Symank, Susan and Larry Terkel, Beth D. Tractenberg, Dwayne Vance, Rhonda Wasserman,Walter A. Wilson III, Suzanne Woo, Jill Zamsky, and Rebecca Zucker.

About the Author

Donna Gerson is the author of *Choosing Small, Choosing Smart: Job Search Strategies for Lawyers in the Small Firm Market* (NALP, 2nd ed. 2005) and is a contributing editor for *Student Lawyer* magazine, an American Bar Association publication, and the author of numerous articles and brochures on legal career issues.

She served as the director of the career services office at the University of Pittsburgh from 1994–2001. Prior to her work in career services, Gerson clerked for a judge and worked in private practice.

Gerson is a member of the American Bar Association, the Pennsylvania Bar Association, and the Allegheny County Bar Association and is licensed to practice law in the Commonwealth of Pennsylvania.

She earned her undergraduate degree from the University of Pennsylvania, her law degree from Temple University, and her master's degree in Library and Information Sciences (MLIS) from the University of Pittsburgh.

A popular speaker at law schools nationwide, Gerson lectures about small firm hiring practices, job seeking strategies for lawyers, and networking skills. She can be reached at donna@donnagerson.com.

About NALP

NALP – The Association for Legal Career Professionals – is a non-profit association of law schools and legal employers. Founded in 1971 as the National Association for Law Placement, NALP is dedicated to facilitating legal career counseling and planning, recruitment and retention, and the professional development of law students and lawyers. To that end, NALP has published numerous resources for job seekers as well as for career services, legal recruitment, and lawyer professional development administrators and also distributes additional resources from other publishers. For information on resources currently available from NALP, visit the online bookstore at **www.nalp.org**. NALP's website also features research findings, including national summaries of the annual NALP *Associate Salary Survey*, and other information relevant to J.D. job seekers. NALP also hosts three additional websites – **www.nalpdirectory.com**, the online *NALP Directory of Legal Employers*; **www.nalplawschoolsonline.org**, The online *NALP Directory of Law Schools*; and **www.pslawnet.org**, NALP's Public Service Law Network, which offers an online database listing paid and unpaid internships, fellowships, and professional positions.